Georgia "In-Brief"®

Distinctions between Federal and State law

Glenn R. Riser

Jackson Lee Todd

November 5, 2016

ISBN- 13: 978-1540416629

ISBN- 10: 1540416623

The information provided within this book is for general informational purposes only. There are no representation or warranties, express or implied, about the completeness, accuracy, reliability, suitability or availability with respect to the information, products, or related graphics contained in this book for any purpose. Credit for any source materials used in developing my personal notes, used to create this book, are included in the References Section to ensure transparency and accountability. Use this information at your own risk. The unauthorized reproduction or distribution of this copyrighted work is illegal. Please excuse any typographic errors.

***To our Dads**,*

who we have trusted each step of the way,

and who might still be the coolest guys ever.

Contents

Introduction 8

A note on the Georgia Bar Exam 8

    Essay 9

    MPT 9

    MBE 9

    MPRE 9

1. Property (MBE and State Bar Tested) 11

    1.1 Introduction 11

    1.2 Georgia Property Distinctions 11

    1.3 Key Take-Aways 17

2. Constitutional Law (MBE and State Bar Tested) 19

    2.1 Introduction 19

    2.2 Georgia Constitutional Law Distinctions 19

    2.3 Key Take-Aways 22

3. Civil Procedure (MBE and State Bar Tested) 23

    3.1 Introduction 23

    3.2 Georgia Civil Procedure Distinctions 23

    3.3 Key Take-Aways 29

4. Criminal Law & Procedure (MBE and State Bar Tested) 31

    4.1 Criminal Law 31

    4.1.1 Introduction 31

    4.1.2 Georgia Criminal Law Distinctions 31

    4.1.3 Key Take-Aways 36

    4.2 Criminal Procedure 37

    4.2.1 Introduction 37

    4.2.2 Georgia Criminal Procedure Distinctions 37

    4.2.3 Key Take-Aways 39

5. Contracts; Commercial Paper and Secured Transactions (MBE and State Bar Tested) 41

    5.1 Contracts 41

    5.1.1 Introduction 41

    5.1.2 Georgia Contracts Distinctions 41

    5.1.3 Key Take-Aways 42

    5.2 Commercial Paper 44

    5.2.1 Introduction 44

    5.2.2 Georgia Commercial Paper Distinctions 44

5.2.3 Key Take-Aways 45

5.3 Secured Transactions 46

5.3.1 Introduction 46

5.3.2 Georgia Secured Transactions Distinctions 46

5.3.3 Key Take-Aways 48

6. Torts (MBE and State Bar Tested) 50

6.1 Introduction 50

6.2 Georgia Torts Distinctions 50

6.2.1 Negligence 50

6.2.1.1 Standards of Care 50

6.2.1.2 Statutory Standards 51

6.2.1.3 Negligent Infliction of Emotional Distress 52

6.2.1.4 Causation 52

6.2.1.5 Damages 52

6.2.1.6 Defenses 53

6.2.2 Strict Liability 53

6.2.3 Vicarious Liability 54

6.2.4 Intentional Torts 54

6.2.5 Defamation 55

6.2.6 Invasion of Privacy 55

6.3 Key Take-Aways 56

7. Evidence (MBE and State Bar Tested) 58

7.1 Introduction 58

7.2 Georgia Evidence Distinctions 58

7.3 Key Take-Aways 59

8. Business Organizations (State Bar Tested) 60

8.1 Business Associations 60

8.1.1 Introduction 60

8.1.2 Business Associations 60

8.1.3 Key Take-Aways 63

8.2 Partnerships 63

8.2.1 Introduction 63

8.2.2 Partnerships 64

8.2.3 Key Take-Aways 66

8.3 Corporations 67

8.3.1 Introduction 67

8.3.2 Corporations 67

8.3.3 Key Take-Aways 72

9. Family Law (State Bar Tested) 75

    9.1 Introduction... 75

    9.2 Family Law (State Bar Tested) 75

    9.3 Key Take-Aways 79

    9.4 Introduction to Delinquency and Dependency 80

    9.5 Delinquency 81

    9.6 Dependency... 82

    9.7 Delinquency and Dependency Key Take-Aways 85

10. Trusts, Wills, and Estates (State Bar Tested).. 88

    10.1 Introduction... 88

    10.2 Trusts, Wills, and Estates.. 88

    10.3 Key Take-Aways 93

11. Non-Monetary Remedies (State Bar Tested).. 97

    11.1 Introduction... 97

    11.2 Things to Know.. 97

    11.3 Key Take-Aways 99

12. Professional Responsibilities (Ethics) (MPRE and State Bar Tested)................. 100

    12.1 Introduction... 100

    12.2 Professional Responsibilities 100

    12.3 Key Take-Aways 101

Conclusion 102

References... 103

Exhibits 105

    Exhibit 1: Rule Against Perpetuities Chart... 106

    Exhibit 2: United States Constitution Quick Reference 107

    Exhibit 3: Agency and Partnership Table 113

    Exhibit 4: MRPC Professional Responsibilities Rules Table 114

Glossary 123

About the Authors... 130

Foreword

The source of materials for this work was our personal notes taken while in law school and while attending Barbri lectures in preparation for the bar examination, and relevant Georgia statutes and scholarly works. We have included references for pertinent topics to ensure transparency and accountability.

This text is specifically focused upon what may appear on the Georgia bar examination. For more comprehensive coverage of Federal law you may reference *Law School "In-Brief"* (*"LSIB"*) for a description of the core courses in Federal law accompanied by pivotal case summaries in each section.

In our opinion, *Law School "In-Brief"* and *Georgia "In-Brief"* provide the requisite information necessary to pass the MBE and Georgia portions of the bar, and are specifically targeted to do so. *A Foundation in Law "In-Brief"* is more tailored to current law students who are in the process of taking the core courses in Federal law.

These texts should serve as "bibles" for law students to form a nucleus of information that can be converted into any learning style. We hope to complete texts for each State to address distinctions between Federal and specific State law.

Georgia "In-Brief": Distinctions between Federal and State Law

Introduction

This book is specifically focused on students in law school that are planning to take the Georgia bar examination. The sections that follow address the distinctions between Federal and State law of Georgia. Understand that the Georgia bar exam is not simply a test of State law distinctions, yet understanding the distinctions is important.

You may notice that some chapters are relatively brief, but don't assume their substance is any less important because of it. We decided to keep a few of the doctrinal sections like Contracts and Evidence rather short as the distinctions between Federal and Georgia law are few. Note that we deviated from this rule with non-doctrinal ("elective") classes like Family Law, Business Organizations, and Trusts, where the text is largely identical to what is found in *LSIB* with a few minor relevant changes. Our reasoning is thus: we assume students already have a sound bearing with the doctrinal classes, and in case the elective course material is unfamiliar during the initial bar prep period, this text should easily explain the new concepts for those students. It is our hope that this format will keep the text to a manageable length. It is important to remember that this is not a cumulative text. Much like *LSIB*, this book presents the important rules and distinctions more likely to appear on the Georgia bar exam. If in your studies you discover that we should include something new, please let us know.

A note on the Georgia Bar Exam

The Georgia Bar Exam is a two day examination, with each day totaling six hours. Day one consists of two parts: the essay portion consists of four 45 minute essay questions, and the Multistate Performance Test ("MPT") section consists of two 90 minute MPT questions. Day two consists of the Multistate Bar Examination Section ("MBE") which is 200 multiple choice questions.

Essay

The Essay Portion consists of all MBE subjects plus Business Organizations; Commercial Paper & Secured Transactions; Family Law; Federal Practice & Procedure; Georgia Practice & Procedure; Non-Monetary Remedies (sometimes called "Equity"); Ethics; and Trusts, Wills, & Estates. Please refer to *LSIB* for coverage of Federal Practice and Procedure.

MPT

The MPT examines fundamental lawyering skills. The six skills are: 1) problem solving; 2) legal analysis and reasoning; 3) factual analysis; 4) communication; 5) organization and management of a legal task, and 6) recognizing and resolving ethical dilemmas. For more information on this exam, consult the National Conference of Bar Examiners ("NCBE") website.

MBE

The MBE covers the following subjects: Constitutional Law; Contracts; Criminal Law and Procedure; Civil Procedure; Evidence; Property; and Torts. Again, consult the NCBE website for a very helpful MBE subject matter outline. Its guidelines for areas of study will, if used properly, provide a nice strategy toward exam prep. *LSIB* includes both a strategy and a tactical plan for MBE studies.

MPRE

In addition to passing the bar exam, the state of Georgia requires each applicant to complete the Multistate Professional Responsibility Exam. This exam is administered separately from the bar exam, and consists of 60 multiple choice questions in two hours. A scaled score of

75 is required in Georgia. Again, consult the NCBE website for more information. The MPRC

Professional Responsibilities Chart, in Exhibit 4, includes the subject matter tested on the MPRE.

1. Property (MBE and State Bar Tested)

1.1 Introduction

The key concepts covered in Property Law include: land sale contracts; deeds as conveyances of property; the concept of a marketable title; misrepresentation; recording; landlord and tenant duties; tenancies; easements; real covenants; ownership tenancies; waste; present possessory estates; future interests in property, and mortgages. Also you should briefly consider the rule against perpetuities (See Exhibit 1) and adverse possession. Understand the Federal law, as there is a significant overlap between topics tested on the MBE and State bar examination.

1.2 Georgia Property Distinctions

Land Sale Contract: A land sale contract is where the seller holds the deed to the property until all of the payments have been made. Once payments have been made the seller should convey the deed to the buyer. If payments are not made the buyer is subject to foreclosure in a manner similar to a title theory State. Standard defenses for a land sale contract are contract formation, contract defenses, and damages.

Deeds: Real property is conveyed by deed. Deeds must be in writing, signed by the grantor, and comply with Statute of Frauds requirements (same as the common law (CL) plus two subscribing witnesses). The deed must reasonably identify the parties and land. Know the types of deeds: general warranty, special warranty and quit claim. General warranty is the best type as it warrants clear title from the original date of conveyance. Special warranty only warrants that the title is clear for the time that the seller owned it, not before. Quit claim warrants that the seller is conveying his interest (which may include encumbrances) and is the least preferable type of deed.

Marketable Title: There is no implied warranty of title in Georgia. It is up to the buyer to investigate whether the title to a property is marketable (i.e. free from liens and other encumbrances) at closing. Watch out for defects in the chain of title.

Misrepresentation: Misrepresentation includes a seller's failure to disclose; active concealment of a material defect; and fraud. A seller can be liable for defects if: the seller knew or had reason to know of a defect; the defect is not obvious or visible and the seller does not think the buyer will discover through an ordinary inspection; or the defect is material and the buyer would not have been induced to buy if he had known about it. This is referred to as failure to disclose. Active concealment is when the seller actively takes measures to conceal a defect, like painting over water marks in a ceiling, or patching and painting wood trim that has wood destroying organism damage. Fraud occurs when the seller makes false statement of fact to the buyer, whether or not the statement is actually false or negligent. The buyer must have been induced to buy the property based on the false statement and the statement must have a material effect on the property. Like when a buyer asks, "Has the roof ever leaked?" If the seller in this example who painted over water marks in the ceiling replies, "No, the roof has never leaked," the statement is obviously false. If the buyer relies on the fact that the roof never leaked, the cost of repairing the roof is material, thus having a material effect.

Recording Acts: Georgia is a RACE-NOTICE jurisdiction for recording purposes. Under this type, priority is given to the party who first recorded if that party had no notice of prior unrecorded claims to the same property. There are three types of notice: actual (learned from a source); record (a prior deed was evidenced in the chain of title); and inquiry (where the buyer should have inspected the property).

Landlord/Tenant: A landlord has a duty to conduct reasonable inspection and maintain the property to ensure that it is habitable. The implied warranty of habitability applies. A landlord also has a duty to deliver possession upon completion of a valid transaction. A commercial tenant must remove trade fixtures prior to vacating the premises otherwise they will be considered abandoned and become the property of the landlord.

Tenancies: There are four types of tenancies (residential and nonresidential): a tenancy for years; a periodic tenancy; a tenancy at will; and a tenancy at sufferance. A tenancy for years runs for a specific time and terminates automatically at the end of the time, e.g. a lease. A periodic tenancy continues for set periods of time, e.g. month-to-month. If notice is not given prior to the end of the lease it will automatically renew for the set period of time. Month-to-month would be renewed for one month. Year-to-year would be renewed for one year. Where no time is specified for the termination of a tenancy, the law construes it to be a tenancy at will. Sixty days' notice from the landlord or thirty days' notice from the tenant is necessary to terminate a tenancy at will.

A tenancy at sufferance, sometimes called a holdover, is when a tenant stays in possession longer than permitted. A tenancy at sufferance lasts until a landlord takes steps to evict the tenant. A landlord is not allowed to use self-help to evict a tenant in Georgia, like changing the locks or turning off the power, and must give notice and file an action ("writ of possession") in court in order to evict. The award will be foreseeable damages. In Georgia, a landlord is not required to mitigate damages.

Easements: An easement is an interest to use land possessed by another or to restrict the use of another's land. There are four types of easements: implied easement by necessity; statutory easement by necessity; easement by prescription; and a negative easement. An implied easement by necessity is when a parcel of land is sold (where unity of ownership existed), and the parcel becomes landlocked with no alternative ingress to or egress from the property. In this case, an easement to either leave or enter the property is implied. In Georgia, the implied easement must reasonably be necessary for the use or enjoyment of the landlocked property. For a statutory easement by necessity, no unity of ownership is required. Land that is used for residential or agricultural purposes must be landlocked with no ingress to or egress from the land and the owner of the servient estate generally is paid compensation. An easement by prescription is similar to adverse possession. While adverse possession is for ownership; an easement by prescription is for usage. Don't get tripped up. An easement by prescription must be open and notorious; adverse and hostile; and continuous for twenty years for wild lands, or seven years for improved lands. The usage does not need to be exclusive and tacking may be applied. A negative easement (sometimes called a restrictive covenant) is generally a requirement not to do something on the land. When a parcel is purchased the negative easement runs with the land unless the buyer is a BFP without notice.

Real Covenants: A real covenant is a written promise either to do or not to do something on the land. Generally the real covenant runs with the land if it is in writing; the parties intended future parties to be bound; horizontal privity exists between the original parties; vertical privity exists between an original party and a future party; the covenant touches and concerns the land; and the future party has notice. Remedies are often injunctive relief or damages. For example, if someone builds a house that violates a real covenant, a court may not find it equitable to have them tear down the house, or prevent them from completing the home if it is nearly completed, but the court may assess damages to be paid to the affected parties. An equitable servitude is the same as a real covenant but there are no privity requirements and the remedy generally is an injunction.

Ownership Tenancies: In Georgia, there are two types of ownership tenancies: joint tenancies and a tenancy in common. Georgia does not recognize tenancy by the entirety. Under a joint tenancy each owner has an undivided interest in the entire estate with the right of survivorship. Joint tenants must have identical interests; from the same conveyance; they must take at the same time and have equal rights to possession. Under a joint tenancy the right of survivorship can be severed and converted to a tenancy in common by: a conveyance by one joint tenant; mutual agreement; murder of one joint tenant by another; simultaneous deaths of the joint tenants; or by partition. Under a tenancy in common, each owner has an equal share of ownership in the property without the right of survivorship, e.g. one-half interest, and can be extinguished by partition.

Waste - Usually the life tenant maintains the property. Waste is an affirmative action that causes harm to the property. Ameliorative waste increases the value of the property, such as improvements to the property. Permissive waste is a failure, physically or financially, to maintain the property. The tenant must make repairs and pay taxes and interest on the mortgage. Voluntary waste is a structural change that harms the property or depletes resources on the property. Resources may be depleted if the property was already being used for that purpose.

Present possessory estates – In Georgia, present possessory freehold estates include fee simple and life estate. Georgia has abolished fee tail. Present possessory non-freehold estates include landlord-tenant estates.

Future Interests – Future interests held by a grantor include: a reversion; the possibility of reverter; and a right of entry. Future interests held by a grantee include a remainder and an executory interest.

Mortgages - Mortgages are security interests in land. They are the union of two elements: debt and a voluntary lien. They must be in writing per the SOF. Debtor = mortgagor, creditor = mortgagee. The majority theory (majority of the States, including Georgia) is the lien theory where the mortgagor has title and the right to possession absent foreclosure, and the mortgagee has a lien. The mortgagor has possession until a foreclosure action is completed. The minority theory (minority of the States) is the title theory, which is where the mortgagee has title to the property, not the mortgagor. In some States a mortgagee can go into possession upon default (intermediate theory) and remain during foreclosure. Foreclosure is when a mortgagee can satisfy debt through judicial action. Georgia, however, does not require judicial action. A lender is not required to obtain a court decree before foreclosing. Sales proceeds from foreclosures pay off mortgages in order of priority. Each claimant is entitled to satisfaction in full. If proceeds are less than the debt, the mortgagee can seek a default judgment against a defaulting mortgagor.

Redemption in equity (majority theory/Georgia) is when a mortgagor can redeem property by paying the amount due prior to foreclosure. Statutory redemption (minority theory) is where a mortgagor may redeem property after the foreclosure, which is allowed by some States. Creditors must record their interests and take priority in the order recorded. Purchase money mortgages are senior to all other interests and are mortgages exchanged for money to buy property. A junior interest (an interest recorded later) is terminated by foreclosure of superior claims. A senior interest is unaffected by a junior interest foreclosure. A due-on-sale clause, often contained in mortgages, is where the entire note balance must be paid before the seller can convey a deed to a new purchaser.

Rule Against Perpetuities: The Rule against Perpetuities (RAP) is one of the most difficult concepts in property. It is a concept that is meant to keep properties available for purchase and to restrict families from keeping property in the family name for centuries. Please refer to Exhibit 1 which contains a flow chart for deciding if the RAP has been violated.

Adverse Possession: Adverse possession is what it sounds like; taking someone else's property without their permission. It may sound similar to an easement by prescription which we discussed a few paragraphs earlier. The difference between the two is that an easement by prescription is for use, not possession. Adverse possession is for possession (outright ownership), not just use. Adverse possession requires that: the possession be adverse or hostile (without permission); actual possession exists; the possession is open and visible (or notorious); the possession is exclusive; it is continuous; it is held under color of title (pretending to or representing ownership to others); and is held for the statutory period. Each State has its own defined statutory period. In Georgia the period is seven years with written evidence of title, otherwise twenty years.

1.3 Key Take-Aways

a. Georgia is a race-notice State.

b. A landlord is not allowed to use self-help in Georgia to evict a tenant.

c. In Georgia, an implied easement must be reasonably necessary for the use or enjoyment of the landlocked property.

d. Georgia is a lien theory State.

e. The time period for adverse possession in Georgia is seven years with written evidence of

    title, otherwise twenty years.

f. Georgia does not require judicial foreclosure.

2. Constitutional Law (MBE and State Bar Tested)

2.1 Introduction

Constitutional Law permeates many of the other classes you will have in law school. You will see it in Property, Family Law, Criminal Law/Procedure, Civil Procedure, Torts and many other classes. Having a sound understanding of the Constitution is fundamental in studying the different aspects of the law. We have included a quick-reference guide for the Constitution, which can be found in Exhibit 2. The areas that you should be most familiar with for law school and for the bar examination are *italicized* for ease of reference. The ones that are not italicized we did not address in my law school. For more detailed coverage of Federal constitutional law, please reference *Law School "In-Brief"*.

The subtopics that you should know well include: Federal judiciary power; Federal legislative power; Federal executive power; Federalism; the structure of the Constitution; individual liberties; equal protection; and the First Amendment. Georgia distinctions are contained in the following section.

2.2 Georgia Constitutional Law Distinctions

<u>Due Process Clause</u>: The Due Process Clause ("DPC") is important to understand as this claim arises in conjunction with many other areas. Remember to analyze both procedural (the appropriate manner to deal with a case) and substantive (the court's authority to decide the case) due process. Procedural due process ordinarily requires both notice and opportunity to be heard. Georgia's DPC requires a higher standard of review than federal DPC. In Georgia, "sufficient justification" must be shown.

Inherent in the DPC is the fundamental right to privacy, which Georgia recognized in 1904 before any other state. Zoning ordinances (under the state's police powers) do not violate

19

DPC if substantially related to health, welfare, safety, and moral interests. Regulations on businesses, however, need only rational basis scrutiny.

Equal Protection Clause: Georgia's Equal Protection Clause ("EPC") is the same as under the U.S. Constitution.

Freedom of Conscience: Georgia's Constitution separately enumerates a freedom of conscience which creates the right to worship God according to one's own conscience.

Religious Freedom: This area is the same as the U.S. Constitution. Religious beliefs and practices do not exempt conduct required to protect the health, safety, and rights of others.

Freedom of Speech and Press: All subjects of communication are okay, however the communicating party is still liable for abuse of the right. Courts may infringe upon protected expression if: (1) There is an important interest; (2) the government's interest is unrelated to suppression of speech; and (3) the incidental restriction is no greater than necessary.

Georgia includes freedom from prior restraint. Infringement of this right opens the door for libel action, process action, and invasion of privacy. The press has a qualified privilege against disclosure of confidential news sources, though this right is not absolute. The privilege is not available in compelling circumstances.

Protection of Citizens: This clause in the Georgia Constitution is similar to the "Privileges and Immunities" clause of the U.S. Constitution.

Right to Keep and Bear Arms: The General Assembly has the power to ascribe the *manner* in which arms may be regulated (e.g. the state may limit certain types of firearms, say, sawed-off shotguns).

Right to Assemble and Petition: Same as U.S. Constitution.

Legislative Power: Georgia's General Assembly is composed of a Senate of no more than 56 persons and a House of Representatives of no fewer than 180 persons.

Enactment of Laws: All bills of revenue or appropriations must originate in the House, be limited to a single subject or single matter. A bill becomes law with a majority vote. All acts must be signed by the president of the Senate and speaker of the House. If a bill is rejected by either House it may not again be proposed during the same session absent consent of two-thirds of the rejecting body. A law not signed by the Governor within six days becomes law unless during those six days the General Assembly adjourns for a period more than forty days. At this point, the Governor has forty days to approve or deny the law.

Exercise of Power: This is similar to the "Necessary and Proper" clause of the U.S. Constitution. The government has specific powers: (1) restrictions on land use to protect natural resources or the environment; (2) militia powers and trial by courts-martial; (3) authority of the General Assembly to participate in federal programs or to comply with federal laws; (4) emergency powers; (5) authority of the state to maintain tourism facilities; and (6) control and regulation of outdoor advertising facilities adjacent to federal and interstate highways.

Laws of general nature apply uniformly throughout the state. Local or municipal laws may not be enacted if a general law already exists except as may be authorized by the General Assembly in circumstances not conflicting with general laws.

Taxing: The state may tax by general laws and then only for public purposes. Taxes must be uniform upon the same classes of subjects (tangible personal property, e.g. motor vehicles) within the territorial limits of the taxing authority. Tax revenue goes to the state's general fund. Generally, there are no exemptions on taxes, though local authorities may approve an exemption by a majority referendum. One example, a homestead exemption, may be granted through local law with approval of a majority of electors residing within the local taxing jurisdiction.

Impeachment Powers: The House votes to impeach, and trial by the Senate is presided over by the Chief Justice of the Georgia Supreme Court.

Executive Branch: The Governor has executive powers, law enforcement powers, may act as commander-in-chief of the guard, veto power, may fill vacancies in the House and Senate, and make appointments.

2.3 Key Take-Aways

a. The State of Georgia must show "sufficient justification" for violations of its Due Process clause.

b. The right to privacy is in the state constitution.

c. The freedom of conscience creates a right to worship God according to one's own conscience.

d. Georgia's General Assembly is composed of no more than 56 Senators and no fewer than 180 Representatives.

e. Know the process for enactment of laws.

f. Know the difference between general and local or municipal laws.

g. The state may tax for public purposes. Generally, there are no exemptions on taxes except by majority referendum by local taxing authority.

3. Civil Procedure (MBE and State Bar Tested)

3.1 Introduction

Civil procedure is based on the Federal Rules of Civil Procedure (FRCP). The key concepts you will need to know for Federal law are: jurisdiction, personal and subject matter; pre-trial activities relating to the commencement of an action; trial and post-trial activities; and appeals. Please refer to *Law School "In-Brief"* for a summary of Federal civil procedure. The Georgia Rules of Civil Procedure are reflected in the sections that follow.

3.2 Georgia Civil Procedure Distinctions

Jurisdiction: Personal jurisdiction is over the parties, and requires that: (1) defendant is present in Georgia when served with process (presence); (2) defendant is domiciled in Georgia; (3) defendant is incorporated in Georgia; or (4) by the long-arm statute (operating a business or having an office in Georgia, tortuous act in Georgia, tortuous injury outside Georgia if tort-feasor regularly conducts himself in Georgia, owns property in Georgia, domestic actions with matrimonial domicile in Georgia, any person subject to exercise of jurisdiction of a Georgia court regarding domestic-relations issues).

Venue: Venue, generally, is the defendant's county of residence. If the defendant resides in another county, venue is proper only if he is a joint obligor, joint tort-feasor, joint promisor, co-partner, or joint trespasser. Venue may be transferred if an impartial jury cannot be obtained, or a judge may select a venue if the parties cannot agree.

Service of Process: Service of process requires that a summons and a copy of the complaint are delivered to each defendant. Process may be served by the sheriff or his appointee or any nonparty adult who is appointed by the court. Failure to provide proof of service does not affect validity of service. Service upon a minor age 14 or more may be done by certified or registered mail. The minor then has 60 days to file defensive pleadings. Service may be done by publication for non-residents or unknown claimants to remove a cloud or to quiet title a property. There are other reasons, of course, but just understand that service by publication is generally used for real property/land interests. Defendant must acknowledge or waive service of process by written signature. Waiver must be completed within 30 days, and the defendant still may later object to jurisdiction or venue.

Pleadings: Every pleading must set forth the name of the court and county, the title of the action, the file number, and a description of the type of pleading (e.g. "Reply to Counterclaim").

Complaint: A complaint is a short, plain statement of claim showing that the pleader is entitled to relief, and includes a demand for judgment for the relief. Regarding medical malpractice in which a claim for unliquidated damages is made for $10,000 or less, the pleading shall contain a demand for judgment in a sum certain (e.g. $2,955.00). For damages exceeding $10,000, the demand shall state that the pleader "demands judgment in excess of $10,000.00" with no further monetary amount stated. Special matters (fraud, punitive damages, and special damages) must be pleaded with particularity or specificity.

Defendant's Response: A defendant must file a responsive pleading (motion or answer) within 30 days of service. Motions include: (1) lack of subject matter jurisdiction; (2) lack of personal jurisdiction; (3) improper venue; (4) insufficiency of process; (5) Insufficient service of process; (6) failure to state a claim upon which relief can be granted; and (7) failure to join a necessary party. Motions 2, 3, 4, and 5 are waived if not part of the initial response. Defendant may further file a motion for judgment on pleadings after pleadings are closed, which is treated as a motion for summary judgment. A motion for a more definite statement is intended to correct a vague or ambiguous claim. If the motion is granted and not obeyed within 15 days, the court may strike the pleading to which the motion was directed. A motion to strike is completed within 30 days after service of the pleading, and is intended to remove redundant, immaterial, impertinent, or scandalous claims.

Counterclaim: A counterclaim is filed against an opposing party with the answer. A compulsory counterclaim arises from the same transaction or occurrence as the opposing party's claim, and must be filed in the case. The case will be dismissed if a separate action is filed and the defendant failed to file a compulsory counterclaim. A permissive counterclaim does not arise from the transaction or occurrence, in which case, the person receiving the permissive counterclaim must respond within 60 days.

Cross-claim: A cross-claim is a claim against a co-party arising from the same transaction or occurrence and is never compulsory.

Amending pleadings - A plaintiff has the right to amend once BEFORE the defendant serves his answer. A plaintiff still has the right to amend if defendant has only filed a motion. A motion is not an answer. The defendant has the right to amend once at any time before the entry of a pretrial order. A motion to amend will be granted if there is no right to amend and justice so requires. The opposing party must respond within 15 days of service. A variance is when the evidence at trial does not match what was pleaded.

Discovery: There are five methods to obtain discovery: (1) deposition (written or oral); (2) written interrogatory; (3) production of documents or things, or permission to enter lands for inspection; (4) physical and mental examination; and (5) requests for admission. Any party can use depositions at trial: to impeach the deponent; for an adverse party; when a witness is dead; when witness is out of county; and when witness is unable to attend or is unable to testify at trial.

Depositions require 20 days prior notice to opposing party. If the plaintiff seeks to depose a party prior to expiration of defendant's response time (30 days after service of summons and complaint), plaintiff may do so only with leave of the court. Cross-questions must be served within 30 days upon all other parties. Redirect must be within 10 days. Deponent has 30 days to review the transcript if he so desires.

Scope of Discovery - is anything relevant to the subject matter of the case. If a defendant objects to interrogatories claiming they would be hearsay and not admissible at trial, the objection isn't good because admissibility is not the test. Discovery regarding net worth is relevant if claiming punitive damages. Privileged matter is not discoverable. A responding party must assert privilege. Work product, prepared in anticipation of litigation, is protected. For expert witnesses, if testifying at trial, a party may send interrogatories requesting the expert's name, substance of facts/opinions, and grounds for opinions. If the expert is not expected to testify you can only depose with exceptional need. Enforcement of discovery rules: is affected by seeking a protective order; there is a partial failure (receiving party answers some and objects to others); or total failure (receiving party willfully refuses).

Multiparty Litigation - Proper parties (Permissive Joinder) are parties involved in the action. For a tort case spouses or parents and their children may join. Necessary and indispensable parties are some absentees who ought to be joined because they have some relationship with the action. A necessary party is one, without whom, the court could not accord complete relief, or the absentee would be harmed if she wasn't joined. If a party can't be joined the court must decide whether to proceed without the party or dismiss the whole case at the court's discretion. If the court dismisses the party is called indispensable. Intervention is where an absentee wants to join in a pending action and is allowed in the discretion of the court. An impleader is when a defending party adds a new party, called a third-party defendant. Generally the defending party joins a new party for indemnity. This is often called third-party practice. An interpleader is where one holding money or property (stakeholder) can force all potential claimants into a single lawsuit to avoid multiple litigation and possible inconsistent results. Class actions have four requirements: numerosity, commonality, typicality and adequate representation.

Adjudication: Voluntary dismissal (by plaintiff) requires filing a written notice of dismissal at any time before the first witness is sworn, or filing a stipulation of dismissal signed by all parties who have appeared in the action. Voluntary dismissal (by order of the court): If counterclaim has been pleaded by the defendant prior to the service upon him of plaintiff's motion to dismiss, the action shall not be dismissed against defendant's objection unless the counterclaim can remain pending for independent adjudication by the court. The first voluntary dismissal is without prejudice. Involuntary dismissal is the failure of plaintiff to prosecute or comply with a written court order. After the plaintiff presents evidence in a bench trial, the defendant may move for dismissal on the ground that the plaintiff has shown no right to relief. Involuntary dismissal for failure to prosecute does not act as an adjudication on the merits. Default judgment is automatic if an answer is not filed in time. Default may be opened as a matter of right by filing such defenses within 15 days of default upon payment of costs. If the party is still in default, the plaintiff is entitled to a verdict and judgment by default.

Summary Judgment is granted when the moving party can show that there is no genuine dispute of a material fact and that he is entitled to judgment as a matter of law. You must wait 30 days after commencing an action, or wait until after service of motion for summary judgment by an adverse party. A defending party may move for summary judgment at any time.

Jury Trial: Demand must be in writing and can be withdrawn if the other party agrees. Jury decides questions of damages not equity. In civil cases there are 6 jurors, tough the parties may by written stipulation agree to a smaller jury. Jury can see premises and objects involved in the case if relevant to a just decision. Jury can submit written, unsigned questions directed to witnesses or the court, but for witnesses only after their testimony. If the question is not asked in court the jury is asked to ignore it. If the question asks for admissible information the question is answered by stipulation or additional testimony. If the question is asked of a witness either the court or counsel asks it. Each juror has access to jury instructions. A party can object to jury instructions before the jury is charged or objection is waived

Directed Verdict: Is an exceptional order which takes the case away from the jury. It is moved for after the other side has been heard at trial. Plaintiff moves at the close of all evidence. Denial of the motion does not discharge the jury. The standard is reasonable people could not disagree on the result.

Judgment Notwithstanding the Verdict ("JNOV"): Motion must be made no later than 30 days after entry of judgment. Only a party who has moved for a directed verdict may move to have the verdict and any judgment entered set aside. A motion for new trial may be joined with this motion, or a new trial may be prayed for in the alternative. If a verdict was returned, the court may allow the judgment to stand or may reopen the judgment and either order a new trial or direct the entry of the judgment as if the requested verdict had been directed. If no verdict was returned, the court may direct the entry of judgment as if the requested verdict had been directed or may order a new trial.

Execution of Judgment - Execution is stayed for 10 days after judgment to allow post-verdict motions. The stay pending disposition of such motions is automatic. Stay pending appeal is not automatic.

Relief from Judgment: Accomplished by collateral attack (judgment is void on its face), or direct attack (motion for new trial, motion to set aside). Motion for new trial is based upon an intrinsic defect not on the face of the record or pleadings. Motion to set aside is based upon lack of jurisdiction (personal or subject matter), fraud, mistake, or a defect in the pleadings.

3.3 Key Take-Aways

a. Personal jurisdiction in Georgia is when: defendant is present in Georgia when served, domiciled in Georgia, incorporated in Georgia, or is included in the long-arm statute.

b. Service upon a minor age 14 or more may be done by certified or registered mail. The minor then has 60 days to file defensive pleadings.

c. Waiver of service must be completed within 30 days.

d. Medical malpractice claims for unliquidated damages are made for a sum certain if $10,000 or less, otherwise shall state "demands judgment in excess of $10,000.00".

e. If a motion for more definite statement is granted and not obeyed within 15 days, the court may strike the pleading to which the motion was directed.

f. A motion to strike is completed within 30 days after service of the pleading.

g. A party has 60 days to respond to a permissive counterclaim.

h. An opposing party must respond within 15 days of service of an amended pleading.

i. Depositions require 20 days prior notice to opposing party.

j. Cross-questions must be served within 30 days. Redirect must be within 10 days.

k. Deponent has 30 days to review transcript if he so desires.

l. A necessary party is a party that would be harmed if not joined.

m. An impleader is when a defendant adds a new party for the purposes of indemnification.

n. An interpleader is when a stakeholder can force all potential claimants into a single lawsuit to avoid multiple-litigation.

o. Default judgment occurs when a party fails to respond in time.

p. Default may be opened as a matter of right by filing defenses within 14 days and payment of costs.

q. Six people serve on a jury in civil cases, though parties may agree to fewer by written stipulation.

r. Motion for JNOV must be made no later than 30 days after entry of judgment. If a party didn't move for a directed verdict at trial, they are not allowed to later move for JNOV.

s. Execution is stayed for 10 days after judgment to allow post-verdict motions. This is not automatic for appeals.

t. Relief from judgment is accomplished by collateral or direct attack.

u. Motion for new trial is based upon intrinsic defect no on the face of the record or pleadings.

v. Motion to set aside is based upon lack of jurisdiction, fraud, mistake, or defect in pleadings.

4. Criminal Law & Procedure (MBE and State Bar Tested)

4.1 Criminal Law

4.1.1 Introduction

The key concepts in Criminal Law that you need to know from a Federal perspective include: actus reus and mens rea; common law general and specific intent crimes, malice, strict liability and concurrence; the MPC fault standards; defenses; attempt crimes; responsibility and criminal capacity; common law murder; causation; common law crimes; property and theft offenses; and offenses against the habitation. The key concepts in Georgia Criminal Law that you will need to know include: offenses against habitation; property offenses; stalking; classification of crimes; jurisdiction; mental state; inchoate offenses; responsibility and capacity; offenses against the person; exculpation; sex offenses; and accomplice liability.

4.1.2 Georgia Criminal Law Distinctions

<u>Offenses Against Habitation</u>: Burglary in the first degree is: (1) entering or remaining; (2) within an occupied or unoccupied dwelling house, building or structure; (3) without authority; and (4) with intent to commit a felony or any theft therein. Burglary in the second degree is the same except the building or structure is not designated as a dwelling.

A person commits the offense of home invasion in the first degree when: without authority and with intent to commit a forcible felony therein; and while in possession of a deadly weapon or instrument likely to cause serious bodily injury; he or she enters the occupied dwelling of another. Home invasion in the second degree is the same, except the intent is to commit a forcible *misdemeanor*. Arson is knowingly damaging personal property worth $25 or more by means of fire or explosive.

Property Offenses: Georgia's theft offenses include:

1. <u>Theft by Taking</u>: Taking property unlawfully, or appropriating property, with intent to deprive.

2. <u>Theft by Deception</u>: Obtaining property by deceitful means with intent to deprive.

3. <u>Theft by Conversion</u>: Similar to MBE embezzlement.

4. <u>Theft by Receiving Stolen Property</u>: Receiving, disposing of, or retaining stolen property that he knows or should know is stolen.

5. <u>Theft of Services</u>: When, by deception and with the intent to avoid payment, defendant knowingly obtains services, accommodations, entertainment, or the use of personal property which is available only for compensation.

6. <u>Theft of Lost or Mislaid Property</u>: Person comes into control of property that he knows/learns to have been lost or mislaid and appropriates the property to his own use without first taking reasonable measures to restore the property to the owner.

7. <u>Theft by Shoplifting</u>: With intent to appropriate merchandise for his own use, defendant: (1) conceals or takes possession of merchandise; (2) alters the price tag; (3) transfers merchandise; (4) interchanges the price tag; or (5) wrongfully causes amount paid to be less than merchant's stated amount.

8. <u>Theft by Extortion</u>: Unlawfully obtain property from another person by threatening to: (1) inflict bodily injury to someone; (2) accuse anyone of criminal offense; (3) disseminate bad information about someone; (4) take or withhold action as a public official; (5) bring about or continue a strike/boycott where the property is not obtained for the benefit of the group whose interest the defendant purports to act; or (6) testify or provide information with respect to another's legal claim or defense.

Forgery: is when a person, with intent to defraud, knowingly makes, alters, or possesses any written instrument, other than a check, in a fictitious name, alteration, or purports to be another person.

Stalking: Georgia's stalking statute makes it unlawful for any person to follow, place under surveillance, or contact another person without consent for the purpose of harassment or intimidation. Aggravated stalking involves similar acts in violation of a court order.

Classification of Crimes: Unlike many states, Georgia does not classify crimes into varying degrees of felony or misdemeanor. Punishment is according to individual crimes. A capital felony (murder only) is punishable by death, life imprisonment without parole, or life imprisonment. Life felonies are punishable by (you guessed it!) life imprisonment. Punishment for other felonies and misdemeanors vary depending on the severity of the crime. More serious crimes will result in harsher penalties (prison sentence and/or fines).

Jurisdiction: If a death, the cause of death, or an essential element of the crime causing death occurred in Georgia, Georgia has jurisdiction

Mental State: In Georgia, a person of sound mind and discretion is presumed to intend the natural and probable consequences of his acts but the presumption may be rebutted.

Inchoate Offenses: Georgia follows the common law bilateral ("two guilty minds") approach to conspiracy. Abandonment is a defense to attempt, provided the change of heart was complete and voluntary. Georgia is distinct in that conspiracy *does* merge with the completed crime and attempt.

Responsibility and Capacity: For insanity, a Georgia defendant must prove by a preponderance of the evidence that either: (1) he did not know his act was wrong; or (2) he was operating under a "delusional compulsion." Children under age thirteen cannot be found guilty of a crime in Georgia. Generally, voluntary intoxication is no defense in Georgia.

Offenses Against the Person: Georgia follows the common law rule for murder ("malice aforethought"). Intent to kill can be inferred either by use of a deadly weapon ("deadly weapon rule") or transferred intent. Second degree murder is when defendant causes the death of another human being in the commission of second degree cruelty to children (causing, with criminal negligence, a child under age eighteen excessive physical or mental pain).

A person commits feticide when he causes the death of a fetus at any state of development either: (1) willfully through injury to the mother that would constitute murder if it were to result in the mother's death; or (2) during the commission of a felony. Note that neither abortion doctors (and medical persons providing treatment to a woman) nor the woman herself can be prosecuted for feticide.

Homicide by vehicle is to cause the death of another, without malice aforethought, by driving in a manner that violates the state's motor vehicles and traffic code. Involuntary manslaughter is to kill another person, without any intention to do so, during the commission of an unlawful act other than a felony. Note that Georgia does not follow the common law rule (unintentional killing committed with criminal negligence) or the MPC/modern rule (killing with negligence).

Simple assault is: (1) to commit violent injury; or (2) the reasonable apprehension of immediate violent injury. Aggravated assault is an assault with intent to murder, rape, or rob with a deadly weapon, strangulation device, or discharge of firearm from a vehicle. Simple battery is: (1) intentional physical contact of insulting or provoking nature; or (2) intent to cause harm to another. A person commits aggravated battery by maliciously causing bodily harm through dismemberment, rendering a body part useless, or serious disfigurement. For both simple assault and simple battery, abusive language on the part of the victim, which may provoke the attack, may be a defense to the criminal charges in Georgia. (It may be helpful to remember the sage advice, "Don't let your mouth write a check that your butt can't cash.")

Kidnapping is to abduct or steal away another person without lawful authority and holding such person against his will. Slight movement is sufficient. False imprisonment is to arrest, confine, or restrain a person without legal authority.

Exculpation: Georgia recognizes that deadly force is justifiable for self-defense, defense of others, to prevent a felony in a dwelling, and to prevent a forcible felony (burglary, arson, robbery, sexual battery, aggravated assault and battery, manslaughter, kidnapping, bombing, and felonies involving violence against another person). The privilege is lost if an unlawful weapon is used. A person has no duty to retreat in Georgia.

Sex Offenses: In Georgia, rape is the carnal knowledge of a female forcibly against her will; or a female under age ten. Statutory rape is when the victim is under age sixteen. Uncorroborated testimony of the victim is sufficient to support a rape conviction in Georgia.

Accomplice Liability: An accomplice may be tried and convicted even if the principal is acquitted, convicted of a different crime, or not prosecuted. A party is not an accomplice when his presence, companionship and conduct before and after an offense are not circumstances from which his participation may be inferred.

Georgia does not have a criminal charge identical to common law Accessory After The Fact. Instead, Georgia has various statutory crimes, such as obstruction of justice, harboring a fugitive, or hindering prosecution.

<u>Vicarious Liability</u>: Georgia law will hold a defendant liable for other crimes committed by co-conspirators so long as the other crimes are in furtherance of the objective of the crime and are foreseeable (even if a co-felon is killed).

4.1.3 Key Take-Aways

a. Burglary is more serious if the structure is a dwelling.

b. Home invasion is more serious if intent is to commit a felony.

c. Arson does not need to be a dwelling. Rather, any personal property valued at $25 or more.

d. Know the eight various theft offenses ("Theft by…")

e. Georgia follows the common law bilateral ("two guilty minds") approach to conspiracy.

f. Abandonment is a defense to attempt if complete and voluntary.

g. Conspiracy merges with completed crime and attempt, in Georgia.

h. Georgia follows the "delusional compulsion" test for insanity.

i. Children under age 13 do not have criminal liability.

j. Georgia follows the common law rule for murder ("malice aforethought").

k. Assault and Battery augmented to aggravated status if weapon used.

l. Verbal provocations may be a defense to simple assault or simple battery.

m. Know when deadly force is justified.

n. Defendant is liable for crimes committed by co-conspirators (even if co-felon is killed).

4.2 Criminal Procedure

4.2.1 Introduction

For Criminal Procedure, the key concepts you will need to know in Federal Law include: arrests and detentions; searches and seizures; administrative inspections and searches; and confessions. Criminal Procedure focuses primarily on the 4th, 14th and 5th Amendments and the rules aren't as complex and element-driven as those in criminal law. For Georgia Criminal Procedure you will need to know pre-trial, trial, and post-trial activities.

4.2.2 Georgia Criminal Procedure Distinctions

<u>Pre-Trial</u>: Pre-trial activities are handled in Georgia by superior courts, municipal courts, state courts, and magistrate courts. Superior courts handle felonies and correct errors in courts of limited jurisdiction. Municipal courts handle violations of traffic law and municipal or local ordinances and conduct preliminary hearings. State courts have jurisdiction over entire counties and handle misdemeanors, and preliminary hearings. Magistrate courts cover minor criminal offenses. Pre-trial custody is meant to lessen threats to society; facilitate the judicial process; and keep the accused from escaping.

Upon release, to ensure appearance in court, a clerk can issue a summons or a police officer can issue a notice to appear. Defendants charged with capital or life felonies are not entitled to release. If bail is refused, defendant has a right to a grand jury within 90 days. If the death penalty is sought, defendant may be entitled to one extension up to 90 days. First appearances are held before a neutral judicial officer within 48 hours of arrest or within 72 hours of arrest by warrant. A probable cause determination usually occurs at these hearings. If a demand for a speedy trial is made, the trial must begin during the same or following court term for non-capital offenses, and within two regular court terms for capital offenses. Court terms begin every six months and vary by county.

Georgia recognizes the reciprocal discovery of information rule. Defendants may be required to be: fingerprinted; provide a blood sample; pose for photos or voice identification; and appear in a line-up or dress-up in certain types of clothing. For plea bargains, they must be voluntary, the defendant must consent, and the judge has discretion to either accept or reject the plea bargain. An arraignment is where the defendant pleads guilty, not guilty or *nolo contendere*, and an arraignment can be waived by the defendant. The court sets the date for arraignments, and notice must be given to the parties at least 5 days prior. Pretrial motions must be made within 10 days following arraignment.

Trial: For jury selection there are generally six jurors for a misdemeanor criminal trial and twelve for a felony trial. For misdemeanor trials, the jurors are selected from a panel of twelve. For felony trials, the jury selection is from a panel of 30 (or 42 if the death penalty is sought). Peremptory challenges can be made on any grounds except race, national origin and gender type. Peremptory challenges are limited to fifteen for capital or life felonies, nine for other felonies, and three for misdemeanors. Peremptory challenges are generally per defendant. When trial begins: an opening statement is made after the jury has been sworn in; opening statements are made by the prosecution first and then the defense (defense can wait until it begins its case); the State presents its case; the defense presents its case; and the State may rebut. A charge conference is held without the jury present. Closing arguments are then made. Finally, jury instructions are given by the judge; the jurors deliberate and reach a verdict, which must be unanimous. Additional jury instruction may be given at the judge's discretion, and there must be a verdict on each count.

Post-Trial: Those found guilty of a non-capital offense may generally be released unless it is a felony crime and the person has a prior felony conviction. Motions to arrest ("halt") the verdict must be made during the same term at which judgment was obtained. For sentencing, the jury may decide life or death and it doesn't need to be unanimous in capital cases. Also, courts will not usually pronounce the sentence if the person is incompetent or insane, the defendant has been pardoned, the person is not the person who was convicted, or the defendant is pregnant. Generally, a guideline score sheet is developed for offenses and offenses are scored as either primary or additional, with primary being the most serious.

4.2.3 Key Take-Aways

a. Pre-trial activities are handled in Georgia by superior courts, municipal courts, state courts, and magistrate courts.

b. Georgia court terms begin every six months and vary by county.

c. First appearances are held before a neutral judicial officer within 48 hours of arrest, or within 72 hours of warrant arrest.

d. If bail is refused, defendant has right to grand jury within 90 days. Defendant may receive one 90-day extension if death penalty is sought.

e. Georgia recognizes the reciprocal discovery rule.

f. The court sets the date for arraignments, with notice given at least five days prior.

g. All pretrial motions must be made within ten days following arraignment.

h. There are 6 jurors for misdemeanors and 12 for felonies.

i. Peremptory challenges limited to fifteen for capital or life felonies; nine for other felonies, and three for misdemeanors.

j. Motions to arrest the verdict must be made during the same term at which judgment was obtained.

5. Contracts; Commercial Paper and Secured Transactions (MBE and State Bar Tested)

5.1 Contracts

Georgia generally follows the contract law you learned in school driven by either the UCC or common law. The key concepts for contracts that you need to know are: the governing law; valid contract formation; counteroffers; option contracts; defenses for the enforceability of a contract; breach; anticipatory repudiation; promissory estoppel; damages; the parol evidence rule; remedies for a breach of contract; excusing performance after the contract; warranties; and third parties to a contract. Please refer to *Law School "In-Brief"* for coverage of contract concepts that you will need for the MBE and State bar. Commercial paper and secured transactions are addressed within this section and should be committed to memory for essay purposes. There are a few Georgia distinctions which follow.

5.1.1 Introduction

There are a few distinctions between Contract law as we know it and Georgia law. The few Georgia distinctions follow.

5.1.2 Georgia Contracts Distinctions

Consideration: Georgia follows the minority view that the requirement for consideration is met even if the promisor receives nothing of value from the promisee. It is sufficient that the promise incurs a loss or disadvantage. Additionally, Georgia law distinguishes between "good" and "valuable" consideration. "Good" consideration arises from a natural duty or moral obligation. "Valuable" consideration is, not surprisingly, money.

Georgia allows a substitute for consideration when there is a promise under a seal. The existence of an official seal creates a rebuttable presumption of consideration. Here, there must be a signed writing compliant with the Statute of Frauds.

Statute of Frauds: In Georgia, contracts involving the lending of money, payment of damages, or the revival of debt must be in writing to be enforceable. This is in addition to the normal SOF rule you learned about in first-semester Contracts class.

Interest in Land: Part performance is sufficient to allow full performance of a contract for the sale of land when either: (1) the vender accepted full payment; (2) the vendee is in possession of property and partial payment; or (3) the vendee is in possession of property and has made valuable improvements.

Mitigation of Damages: Georgia does not recognize mitigation of damages for landlords in lease contracts, though mitigation is required for tenants in those contracts. Additionally, there is no duty to mitigate when there is an absolute promise to pay, or when an employee seeks severance payment (because the employer has an absolute duty to pay).

Agency: Georgia follows the Equal Dignity Rule which requires the authority of the agent must be in writing if the SOF requires the instrument to be in writing. If the instrument needs not be in writing, remember the traditional rule of actual or apparent authority.

5.1.3 Key Take-Aways

a. Consideration involves either a benefit or detriment. The promisor need not receive the benefit for consideration to be valid.

b. In addition to the normal Statute of Frauds requirements, Georgia requires contracts involving lending of money, payment of damages, or the revival of debt to be in writing.

c. A landlord has no duty to mitigate in Georgia.

d.   Georgia follows the Equal Dignity Rule.

5.2 Commercial Paper

5.2.1 Introduction

The key concepts relating to commercial paper include: notes; drafts; the parties; order and bearer paper; the concept of negotiability; holders in due course; endorsements; and legal obligations.

5.2.2 Georgia Commercial Paper Distinctions

Article 3 of the UCC governs commercial paper. Georgia incorporates the UCC into GA Code Title 11 Article 3. Commercial paper requires a party to pay money versus deliver goods or services. There are two types of commercial paper: notes and drafts. A note has two parties, a maker and a payee. The maker is the person signing the note and promising to pay and the payee is the person to be paid. A draft has three parties: a drawer, a drawee and a payee. The drawer is the person who signs and orders payment. The drawee is the person who is ordered to make payment, like a bank. The payee is the same as in a note, the person to be paid.

Commercial paper can either be negotiable or non-negotiable. We'll go backwards here. If it is non-negotiable then it is governed by contract law. If it is negotiable it must be: in writing; signed by the maker or drawer; unconditional; a promise or order to pay; a fixed amount; in money; with no other undertaking or instructions; on demand or at a specified time; and made to order or to the bearer. There is no oral commercial paper. A writing cannot be made negotiable by contract or conduct.

Negotiating is the normal way to transfer an instrument (note or draft), but it can also be assigned. An instrument is negotiated by transferring possession and endorsement. Bearer paper requires that payment be made to the bearer, or holder, in physical possession, and can be negotiated solely by transferring possession. Generally, the last endorsement will determine whether the instrument is order paper or bearer paper. Order paper usually states, "Pay to the order of," as you see on your personal checks. Bearer paper is paper that is payable to the bearer or said differently, the one in possession. An instrument is also bearer paper if it does not state a payee.

A holder in due course is: (1) a holder; (2) for value; (3) in good faith; and (4) without notice. This sounds just like a BFP we discussed in the real property section. The Shelter Rule we discussed in the real property section also applies here. The defenses against a holder in due course are: infancy; incapacity, duress, illegality, misrepresentation; discharge in insolvency proceedings; any other discharge the holder has notice of; fraud in the inducement; and fraud in fact.

Signature makes the maker liable or the makers jointly and severally liable. The drawee is obligated to pay according to the terms on the instrument at the time of endorsement. An accommodating party lends his name to another party for signature purposes and is liable in the capacity in which he signed.

Banks must pay out money by following the customer's orders directly otherwise it must re-credit the customer's account. A check is considered stale after six months. Forgery of a payee's name constitutes an invalid negotiation and no one taking the instrument will qualify as a holder.

Each State has (or should have) a prescribed statute of limitations for a claim on a contract, obligation or written instrument.

5.2.3 Key Take-Aways

a. UCC article 3 governs commercial paper.

b. A note has two parties, a maker and a payee.

45

c. A draft has three parties: a drawer, a drawee and a payee.

d. There is no oral commercial paper.

e. Bearer paper requires that payment be made to the bearer.

f. Order paper requires that payment be made to the person to whom payment is ordered, e.g. "Pay to the order of . . ."

g. A holder in due course is: (1) a holder; (2) for value; (3) in good faith; and (4) without notice.

5.3 Secured Transactions

5.3.1 Introduction

The key concepts included in secured transactions are: the security interest; the parties; collateral; security documents; enforcement; purchase money security interests; and priorities.

5.3.2 Georgia Secured Transactions Distinctions

Article 9 of the UCC governs commercial paper. Georgia incorporates the UCC into GA Code Title 11 Article 9. A security interest is an interest in personal property or fixtures that is used to secure the payment or performance of an obligation. Secured transactions usually include: a debtor, an obligor and a secured party. The debtor is the person holding title to the personal property or fixtures. The obligor is the person who has an obligation to pay or perform that is secured by the personal property or fixtures. The secured party is the party having an interest in the secured property. As an example let's say you buy a car from Ford and you finance it from Banker's Bank. Ford is the secured party. Banker's Bank obtains title to the car subject to Ford's security interest, becoming both the debtor and obligor with the car as collateral. When you complete making all of the payments, the car becomes yours, Ford no longer has a security interest, and because Banker's Bank is no longer the debtor or obligor; you would get title. You would also be a debtor to Banker's Bank in this example. You make payments to Banker's Bank while enjoying physical possession and use of the car. We think of this sort of as the title theory in real property, where the bank has title and can foreclose if you default on your payments. A finance company can repossess your car if you stop making payments. They seem similar to us.

Collateral is defined under Article 9 of the UCC as property subject to a security interest or agricultural lien. Article 9 divides collateral into three categories for practical purposes: goods, quasi-tangible property; and intangible property. Goods are considered things that would qualify as movable goods under Article 2 of the UCC. Quasi-tangible property is considered paper, like commercial paper, stocks and bonds, and a letter of credit. Intangible property is considered to be patents, software, accounts, lottery winnings and things of that nature.

Article 9 of the UCC generally addresses two types of documents: security agreements and financing statements. Security agreements are contracts between a debtor and creditor granting a security interest in the collateral, and creating a property right between the debtor and the creditor. A financing statement is a notice that gives the creditor property rights against everyone else. Generally, if you are not in possession or control of the collateral you need a written security agreement.

Enforcement of security agreements is usually achieved by attachment and perfection. Attachment is when the security interest of a creditor becomes effective against the debtor. Perfection is when the security interest of a creditor becomes effective against everyone else. Article 9 of the UCC states that attachment can occur if : (1) value was given; (2) the debtor has the rights in the collateral or the power to transfer rights in the collateral to a secured party; and

(3) there is a security agreement that is written, authenticated by the debtor, and that properly describes the collateral. Perfection must be accomplished by filing the financing statement, having possession, having control and it must be automatic.

A purchase money security interest (PMSI) requires that the collateral being used is a consumer good and is also something sold by a merchant (or financed by a bank). The merchant or bank sells the item to the consumer but retains a security interest in the item being sold. In real property, let's say you finance a dishwasher and install it in your house. The finance company has a PMSI on your dishwasher. You have a mortgage on your house with a bank. You default on your mortgage and the bank takes a foreclosure action. Who owns the dishwasher? It's a fixture in the house. The finance company has an interest because the PMSI creates automatic perfection, protecting the creditor from everyone else. This is called priority. A perfected security interest has priority over an unperfected security interest.

5.3.3 Key Take-Aways

a. UCC Article 9 governs secured transactions.

b. A secured transaction is a security interest in personal property or fixtures.

c. A secured transaction generally has three parties: a debtor; an obligor; and a secured party.

d. Collateral is property subject to a security interest or agricultural lien.

e. Collateral is categorized into three categories: goods; quasi-tangible property; and intangible property.

f. There are two types of secured transactions: security agreements and financing statements.

g. Enforcement of security agreements is usually achieved by attachment and perfection.

h. Perfection is accomplished by filing the financing statement.

i. A PMSI requires that collateral is a consumer good sold by a merchant or financed by a bank.

6. Torts (MBE and State Bar Tested)

6.1 Introduction

The key concepts discussed in this section include negligence, strict liability, vicarious liability, intentional torts, defamation and invasion of privacy. You will notice that this chapter of the book is unique in that it has more sub-headings than most of the other chapters. We did this purposefully to organize the concepts for ease of reference. This section is devoted strictly to the relevant Georgia torts distinctions. For a more broad analysis of torts please consult *Law School "In-Brief"*.

6.2 Georgia Torts Distinctions

6.2.1 Negligence

We have included negligence first, despite the fact that many law school textbooks begin with intentional torts, because of the high frequency of negligence issues on the bar exam. In its most recent MBE outline, the NCBE predicted that one-half of all torts questions are likely to involve issues of negligence.

6.2.1.1 Standards of Care

Premises Liability: Georgia applies the Business Relations Test to distinguish between invitees and licensees. If there is a business relationship between the parties, the injured person is considered an INVITEE and a higher duty of care is owed.

A landowner must exercise reasonable care and refrain from willful and wanton conduct against known trespassers though there is no duty to warn of hidden dangers unless the landowner observes the trespasser in a position of peril. Georgia follows the Firefighter's Rule, though the firefighter can, however, recover as a LICENSEE for injuries caused by negligence unrelated to a fire.

A landlord not in possession is not responsible to third persons for damages resulting from the negligence or illegal use of the property by the tenant.

Automobile Guest Statute: The operator of a motor vehicle owes to passengers the same duty of ordinary care owed to others.

Professionals: Georgia holds professionals to a national standard of care. Under Georgia law, emergency room professionals may be liable for gross negligence, proven by clear and convincing evidence. Georgia does not recognize claims for wrongful birth or wrongful life actions, but does allow actions for wrongful pregnancy/conception.

Rescuers: Under Georgia's Good Samaritan Statute, uncompensated persons ("rescuers") who render aid to victims at the scene of an accident or emergency cannot be held liable for ordinary negligence. Rescuers who act voluntarily must exercise ordinary care.

6.2.1.2 Statutory Standards

Negligence Per Se: Georgia follows the majority rule that violation of statute is negligence per se. Remember, the harm suffered must be of the same type sought to be prevented by the relevant statute.

Dram Shop Act: A person who knowingly furnishes alcoholic beverages to an underage person, or to a noticeably intoxicated person, and who knows that such person is soon likely to drive a car, may be liable for injury or damage caused by the driver to a third person.

6.2.1.3 Negligent Infliction of Emotional Distress

Impact Rule: A plaintiff must demonstrate an impact resulting in physical injury or a type of personal injury, like reputation. Absent personal injury, recovery is allowed only if the defendant's conduct was malicious, willful, or wanton.

Bystanders: Recovery by bystanders is not permitted in Georgia except as between a parent and child when the parent sees their child's suffering or death.

6.2.1.4 Causation

Loss of Chance: If the decedent had an incurable medical condition, causation cannot be established in a failure to diagnose case.

Proximate Cause: Georgia follows the majority view (duty owed to foreseeable plaintiffs), though uses the phrase "ambit of risk" rather than "zone of danger."

6.2.1.5 Damages

Punitive Damages: Recoverable in Georgia if, proven by clear and convincing evidence, defendant's conduct showed willful misconduct, malice, or fraud. Punitive award may not exceed $250,000 except: (1) in a product liability case there is no cap, but only one award may be recovered from a defendant for any single act or omission. Three-quarters of the award must be paid into a state account for the benefit of all plaintiffs; and (2) there is no limit when defendant acted with specific intent to cause harm or was under the influence of alcohol or drugs.

Joint Liability: Georgia follows traditional rules of contribution. When joint liability applies, defendants pay an equal share regardless of their relative degrees of fault. Contribution is prohibited in cases involving moral turpitude.

Indemnity: A passively negligent defendant is allowed to recover indemnification from the actively negligent defendant.

Medical Malpractice Damages: There are caps on recoverable amounts for medical malpractice claims (including wrongful death). A party may not recover more than $350,000 against a single medical facility, or in an award from multiple facilities, the amount from any single facility may not exceed $350,000 and $700,000 from all facilities combined, regardless of the number of facilities in the suit. The aggregate amount of noneconomic damages recoverable shall in no event exceed $1,050,000.

6.2.1.6 Defenses

Contributory Negligence: Plaintiff is barred from recovery if he is contributorily negligent. A child under age six cannot be contributorily negligent. The Last Clear Chance doctrine provides a basis for recovery where a plaintiff is otherwise contributorily negligent.

Comparative Negligence: Georgia is a partial comparative negligence state meaning the plaintiff can recover from the defendant unless her share is equal to or greater than the defendant's share.

Assumption of Risk: In Georgia, the defense of assumption of risk applies when the defendant can show that the plaintiff had: (1) actual knowledge of the danger inconsistent with safety; (2) understanding and appreciation of the risk associated with the danger; and (3) a voluntary exposure to the risk. Assumption of risk may be implied, and, when proved, is a complete bar to recovery.

6.2.2 Strict Liability

Animals: Georgia allows liability for dangerous animals with vicious propensities. It is sufficient to show that the animal was not "at heel or on a leash" in violation of ordinance. The law does not apply to domesticated livestock or (get this!) "domesticated fowl including roosters with spurs." I can only imagine what precipitated this specificity!

Abnormally Dangerous Activities: The only abnormally dangerous activity recognized in Georgia is blasting.

Strict Products Liability: Applies only to new products sold directly from the manufacturer or through a dealer, and the defendant must be the actual manufacturer of the item. Cases must be brought within ten years of the first sale or use of the product.

6.2.3 Vicarious Liability

Parent-Child: Georgia imposes liability on a parent up to $10,000 for a child's willful or malicious injury to a person resulting in medical expenses or destruction of real or personal property.

Tavern keepers: See Section 6.2.1.2 ("Dram Shop Act")

6.2.4 Intentional Torts

Battery: Intent is not part of the prima facie case for battery, though it must be considered in assessing damages. MEDICAL BATTERY may be established by showing that: (1) there was a lack of consent to the procedure performed; or (2) the treatment was at substantial variance with the consent granted.

Defenses to Battery include: SELF-DEFENSE (There is no duty to retreat); DEFENSE OF OTHERS (Georgia follows the "Reasonable Mistake Doctrine"); and DEFENSE OF PROPERTY. Georgia's defense of habitation statute permits a lawful occupant of a home or residence to use deadly force against an intruder when: (1) entry is violent; (2) force used is against a person not a household member; or (3) entry is for purpose of committing a felony and deadly force is necessary to prevent the felony.

Conversion: Damages for the fair market value of the converted property are measured by the highest value existing between the time of conversion and trial. This is a little different from the MBE rule which measures value at time of conversion plus interest at the time of trial.

Intentional Infliction of Emotional Distress: Where physical impact does not occur, Georgia requires the conduct be directed at the plaintiff.

6.2.5 Defamation

Publication: This element requires that the false statement be: (1) heard or read; and (2) comprehended by a third party. Proving the second element is much more difficult to prove, and many questions on the exam hinge on this point. Pay attention.

Radio and Television: Broadcasts by radio and television which are defamatory are actionable in Georgia. If a private individual is defamed, he may recover actual damages if he proves failure to use ordinary care to determine the truth or falsity of the statements. Public officials must prove actual malice.

Truth as Defense: Everyone learns in law school that truth is a defense to defamation suits and Georgia's Constitution specifically so provides. Adding this might earn you an extra essay point. (If you are curious, it can be found in Article 1, Section 1, Paragraph 6.)

6.2.6 Invasion of Privacy

Georgia allows actions for invasion of privacy. There are four types: appropriation, intrusion, public disclosure of private facts, and false light.

6.3 Key Take-Aways

a. Georgia applies the Business Relations Test.

b. Landowner must exercise reasonable care and refrain from willful and wanton conduct against known trespassers.

c. There is no duty to warn of hidden dangers in Georgia unless the landowner observes the trespasser in a position of peril.

d. Georgia follows the Firefighter's Rule, with the exception that a firefighter may make a claim as a LICENSEE for negligence unrelated to a fire.

e. Georgia holds professionals to a national standard of care.

f. Georgia does not recognize claims for wrongful birth or wrongful life, but does allow actions for wrongful pregnancy/conception.

g. Rescuers cannot be held liable for ordinary negligence (Good Samaritan Statute).

h. NIED requires impact, except when defendant is malicious, willful, or wanton.

i. Bystanders cannot recover for NIED unless as between a parent and child.

j. Punitive damages may not exceed $250,000 in Georgia. Know the exceptions to this rule.

k. Know the caps on medical malpractice awards.

l. Georgia is a partial comparative negligence jurisdiction.

m. Georgia allows liability for dangerous animals with vicious propensities.

n. The only abnormally dangerous activity recognized in Georgia is blasting.

o. Strict products liability applies only to new products sold directly from the manufacturer or through a dealer.

p. Georgia imposes liability on a parent for a child's willful or malicious injury to a person.

q. Medical battery may be established by showing that there was a lack of consent to the procedure performed, or the treatment varied substantially from the consent granted.

r. There is no duty to retreat in Georgia.

s. Fair market value is measured by highest value existing between time of conversion and trail.

t. IIED: Georgia requires conduct be directed at the plaintiff if physical impact does not occur.

7. Evidence (MBE and State Bar Tested)

7.1 Introduction

For more complete coverage of this subject, please refer to the latest edition of *Law School "In-Brief"*. This section is tailored to address the distinctions between MBE rules and Georgia evidence law.

7.2 Georgia Evidence Distinctions

Subject	Multistate Rule (MBE)	Georgia Rule (State)
Character Evidence		
To Prove Character	Witnesses may use opinion	Cannot use opinion
How Defendant Proves Character	Personal opinion, but no specific acts	In criminal case, defendant may testify to her own specific acts.
How Prosecution Rebuts	Witnesses for bad reputation or opinion	Reputation, not opinion
Specific Acts	Reasonable notice is required	10 days' notice required to use convictions. No notice required to prove motive.
Rape Shield Acts	Evidence of specific acts admissible to show: (1) defendant not source of physical evidence; (2) sexual behavior of accused; (3) if exclusion of evidence violates defendant's constitutional rights	Sexual behavior of accused only
Impeachment		
Prior Convictions	*Nolo contendere* plea admissible	*Nolo contendere* plea inadmissible to impeach; discharge of finding of guilt under first offender program is inadmissible for general impeachment

Testimonial Evidence

Learned Treatises	Hearsay exception on direct examination.	Admissible only on cross-examination.

Hearsay

Admission	Non-hearsay	Exception to hearsay rule
Prior Consistent Statement	Hearsay	Non-hearsay

Privilege

Accountant-Client	Must be tied to Attorney-Client privilege	Client has right to invoke; confidential communications protected
Doctor-Patient	Not an assumed privilege on MBE	Psychiatrist-Patient Privilege (includes any licensed social worker or professional mental health provider)
Clergy	Recognized	Recognized
Against Self-Incrimination	Testimony	Testimony and tangible evidence
Others	- - - - - - - - - - - - - -	Informant; Marital (Testimony and Communications); Medical Privileges and Confidences; News Reporter's Privilege; Psychotherapist-Patient

7.3 Key Take-Aways

The table above reflects most of the relevant distinctions between State and Federal law for the exam. Georgia underwent its most recent change in evidentiary rules in 2013, changing many formerly distinct rules to be more similar to the Federal Rules of Evidence or what is tested on the MBE. Add this information to the federal law explained in *Law School "In-Brief"* and you should be set for the Georgia bar exam.

8. Business Organizations (State Bar Tested)

"Business organizations," sometimes referred to as "entities" is an umbrella term used to encompass the law courses taught by most law schools. The most common courses are Business Associations, Corporations and Partnerships. These topics have not been tested on the MBE but you will likely see them in your State bar examinations, either in essay or multiple choice form. Try to assimilate the key concepts included here and you'll do well. Post-graduation bar examination study courses present these subjects separately, which we find to be cumbersome. Hopefully, grouping them together will help you in aligning your studies.

8.1 Business Associations

8.1.1 Introduction

The Business Associations course stresses the concept of agency and could be viewed as an overview course for corporations and partnerships as well. So there will be some overlap. We'll try to keep it to a minimum.

The key concepts that will be addressed in this section are agency, the liability of principals and fiduciary relationships, and the duties of corporate officers, directors and other insiders. We have included a small table (Exhibit 3) which organizes some basic concepts of agency and partnership which can be found in the back of this book.

8.1.2 Business Associations

Generally, agency is applied to someone who works for a principal. Not like a principal in school, more like a business owner. Under the agency rule there must be a manifestation of consent that the principal allows someone to act on its behalf subject to the principal's control. An agent can have actual authority, which may be implied or express. Implied authority is achieved through necessity, it can be incidental, through conduct or through custom. Express authority is either written or oral. Actual authority is through the eyes of the agent, meaning that based on some implied or express action, the agent believes he has the authority. Apparent authority is through the eyes of a third party, meaning that someone else believes that the agent has authority. A common example is like when you go to a car dealership and see the guy on the floor with the dealership shirt on, standing next to the manager sign, you think he has the authority to help you, whether he really does or not. The reason actual and apparent authority are important is because they can determine liability of the agent and/or the principal.

In Torts, in Law School "In-Brief," we discussed vicarious liability and I included the *Gatzke* case (*Edgewater Motels, Inc. v. Gatzke*, 277 N.W.2d 11 (Minn. 1979)). In the *Gatzke* case, Gatzke burned down a motel by smoking while he was filling out an expense report and the Court held his employer liable because the expense report was within the scope of his employment. Here, we discuss the liability of a principal to third parties and the fiduciary obligations of agents and partners. First, there is a difference between an employee (often called servant) and an independent contractor. Employees are definitely under the control of their principal. Independent contractors can be under the principal's control if the principal tells the independent contractor when and how to do his work, and provides him with tools to do the work. Generally, if the employee or independent contractor is under the principal's control and a tort is committed within the scope of services, the principal is liable. Agents have a fiduciary duty to their principals. Partners have differing levels of liability and fiduciary relationships, whether they are general or limited partners. (We'll discuss more in the Partnership Section.)

Corporate officers, directors and other insiders owe certain duties to the corporation. These duties are the duty of care, the duty loyalty, the duty of good faith, and the duty of disclosure and fairness. These duties are often referred to as obligations of control. The duty of care requires corporate officers, directors and other insiders to act with due diligence and to manage business affairs as a reasonably prudent person would. It doesn't mean that the person can never make a mistake. As long as the mistake was made after exercising due diligence and acting reasonably prudent a mistake is ok. Otherwise there would be no profits and losses, there would only be profits. The duty of loyalty requires that officers, directors and other insiders act in the best interest of the corporation. The duty of good faith is subjective in that its definition is often determined by a jury relying on the reasonability factor. This carries some weight when you consider that generally only persons who act in good faith are indemnified from paying legal expenses personally. The duty of disclosure and fairness deals with trading in corporate securities and the internal actions of officers, directors and other insiders. Essentially, the duty of disclosure can be categorized into that which is said to those outside of the corporation and that which is said to those inside the corporation. Since public corporations have stock that is publicly traded, it is important that what a corporation or its representatives disclose to the public must be truthful and fair. Since internal officers, directors and other insiders have both a fiduciary duty and a duty of loyalty it is important that what they say to internal players is truthful and fair. If a member of the public purchases stock based on false information, the corporation providing the information is subject to civil liability and may be in violation of securities laws enforced by the Securities and Exchange Commission (SEC). If an officer, director or other insider makes a business decision to benefit himself at the expense of the corporation by providing false information or by omitting information he could be terminated and subject to civil liability. These duties are important controls to ensure the integrity of corporations.

8.1.3 Key Take-Aways

a. The agency rule requires that there is a manifestation of consent that a principal allows someone to act on his behalf, subject to his control.

b. Actual authority is implied or express.

c. Actual authority is through the eyes of the agent, not the principal.

d. Apparent authority is through the eyes of a third party.

e. Independent contractors can be considered employees if the principal tells them "how" to do their work.

f. Corporate officers, directors, and other insiders owe the duties of: care; loyalty; good faith; disclosure and fairness to the corporation. They also have a fiduciary duty.

g. If a member of the public purchases stock based on false information the corporation could be in violation of SEC rules and regulations.

8.2 Partnerships

8.2.1 Introduction

Partnerships are generally two or more persons that co-own a business for profit. General partnerships were tradition years ago, but in many instances have been replaced by various forms of partnerships with a single goal of minimizing or eliminating the liability of the partners, whether general or limited, for the acts of the partnership. Partners are generally liable for their own tort actions, unless the actions were taken within the scope of the business, which may save them from liability. Partnerships address all of the bobbing and weaving that people do when they form a co-owner relationship. They are tested on the State bar examination multiple choice portion.

The key concepts addressed in this section are the formation of partnerships; partnership property; the rights of a partner; the partnership agreement; the liabilities of partners; dissolving and winding up partnerships; and the different types of partnerships. We tried to keep it brief.

8.2.2 Partnerships

A general partnership is an association of two or more persons carrying on as co-owners of a business for profit, whether they intend to form a partnership or not. In order to determine if a partnership exists there are three factors to consider: capital investment; control; and profits. A partnership doesn't require a written agreement. A partnership can register with the State, but if no partnership is registered the parties may still be liable if third parties relied upon them as a partnership (apparent authority).

Partnerships acquire property in the name of the partnership. In order to determine if property is partnership property you must: determine if the property was purchased in a partner's name or in the partnerships name; or, if the partnership paid for it it's presumed to be partnership property. If purchased in a partner's name without the use of partnership funds it's generally the partner's property. The partnership can use the property for whatever it wants, but the partner can only use it for partnership purposes, unless the other partners consent to the personal use.

A partner has a right to receive his fair share of profits and can transfer his interest in the partnership like any other financial asset. However, the transfer does not confer any rights to the partnership, only the share of profits transferred. Partners share profits and losses equally.

In a partnership, the partnership agreement generally controls and it usually establishes: compensation; management rights (voting); the right to indemnification; duties; the right to inspect the books; the admission of new partners; and former partner's liability. Generally there is no "right" to compensation. Management rights (voting) are generally determined by the percentage of ownership. As we mentioned earlier the agreement usually includes a right to indemnification as long as the party acted in good faith. The duties in a partnership are similar to those discussed for a corporation and include duties of: care; loyalty; good faith and fair dealing; and information. Partners have a right to inspect the books of the partnership within reason. The admission of new partners is usually based on a vote, and unanimous consent is required. Former partners remain on the hook for liabilities unless the creditor agrees to release him. Dissociation is when a partner ceases to be part of the organization. This can be because: a partner expresses the desire to withdraw; the occurrence of an agreed-upon event; expulsion, bankruptcy, death or incapacity; termination of a partnering business entity; or distribution of all of a partner's interest in the partnership.

For dissolution and winding up of the partnership certain events require dissolution, such as: an event specified in the partnership agreement requires it to wind up at a certain time; an event occurs making it unlawful to continue; a judicial decree; notice of express intent in a partnership at will; or if the partnership is formed to accomplish a defined term or specific task. When a partnership is dissolved the assets are distributed first to the creditors (including partners who have loaned the company money) and second to partners for what is in their capital accounts.

There are different kinds of partnership besides a general partnership. A Limited Liability Partnership (LLP) is just like a general partnership, except a partner in an LLP is not liable for any LLP obligations other than his own torts or those of someone under his direct control. The LLP is liable for torts committed within the scope of its business (vicarious liability again). Limited Partnerships (LP) is a partnership consisting of one or more general partners and one or more limited partners. A limited partner in an LP is not personally liable for the debts of the LP even if he participates in the control of the LP. A Limited Liability Limited Partnership (LLLP) is just like a limited partnership except for the liability. General and limited partners are protected in an LLLP. Limited Liability Companies (LLC) are formed and managed by managers or members in proportion to their profit shares unless specified in an operating agreement. Members get limited liability except for their own torts, as do managers. The LLC is liable for torts committed within the scope of its business and in contracts executed on behalf of the business.

8.2.3 Key Take-Aways

a. A general partnership is where two or more persons are carrying on as co-owners of a business for profit.

b. The three factors needed to determine if a partnership exists are: capital investment; control; and profits.

c. Partnership property may only be used for partnership purposes, unless the other partners consent to other usage.

d. Partners share profits and losses equally.

e. A partner has the right to receive his fair share of the profits and may transfer his interest, but his transfer does not confer any other rights to the partnership other than financial distribution.

f. A partnership generally controls the partnership, and establishes: compensation; voting rights; the right to indemnification; duties; the right to inspect the books; the admission of new partners; and former partner's liability.

g. Voting rights are generally determined by percentage of ownership.

h. When a partnership is dissolved proceeds are distributed first to creditors (including

partners who have loaned the partnership money) and second to partners based on their

capital accounts.

i. The LLP, LP, LLLP and LLC are all forms of partnerships with varying degrees of

liability for the partners.

8.3 Corporations

8.3.1 Introduction

Corporations are business entities that generally have a board of directors, officers and

shareholders. Publicly traded corporations are more restricted in their dealings than private

corporations. Corporations are generally more formal than partnerships. We have attempted to

include only those things in this section that have an inkling of probability that they may be

tested on your State bar examination. This has not been tested on the MBE to date!

The key concepts included in this section are: corporation formation; the selling of

shares; the requirements and duties of directors, officers and shareholders; voting; inspection of

the books; distributions; non-profit corporations; mergers and share exchanges; dissolution; and

Federal securities law.

8.3.2 Corporations

In order to form a corporation, articles of incorporation must be filed with the State and

organizational meetings must be held. Articles of incorporation generally include: the name and

address of the corporation; the name and address of each incorporator; the name and address of

the registered agent; and the number of authorized shares. A de jure corporation is a duly formed

corporation in accordance with the law, and is required to file an annual report or risk administrative dissolution. A de facto corporation is a good faith attempt to form a corporation and an act on the corporation's behalf. This would be like a promoter going out and landing a big contract and then forming a corporation to perform the contract. The promoter would remain liable until the newly formed corporation assumed his role through a novation. Corporations usually create by-laws for administrative matters, but if they conflict with the articles of organization, the articles rule. Foreign corporations are corporations formed under the jurisdiction of another State and must qualify in the State where they wish to conduct business.

When a corporation sells its own shares it is called issuance. Issued shares are the number of shares the corporation actually sold. Outstanding shares are the issued shares that the corporation has not reacquired. Subscriptions are written offers to buy stock from the corporation and are enforceable once the corporation's board accepts them. The corporation can sell the shares to someone else if the subscription is not paid for in 20 days. Consideration is what the corporation receives when it issues stock and can be any tangible or intangible property or benefit to the corporation. Par value is the minimum issuance price, not the fair market value. Watered stock is stock that is purchased for less than par value. Treasury shares are shares that are reacquired by the corporation and may be cancelled or resold for any price as par value prices don't apply to shares that have already been issued. Preemptive rights allow a shareholder to maintain his interest in the corporation when new shares are issued for money to protect against dilution.

There are generally statutory requirements for directors and officers. For directors they must be one or more natural persons 18 years or older. Shareholders elect directors at the annual meeting and shareholders may remove directors with or without cause unless otherwise specified. Vacancies on the board may be filled by directors or shareholders unless specified otherwise. Meetings are required absent the unanimous consent of the directors, notice of the

meeting must occur, and a quorum must exist. A quorum of directors on the board is a majority

unless otherwise specified. The minimum is generally one-third. For voting, the affirmative vote

of a majority of directors present is needed, again, unless otherwise specified.

Directors set policy, supervise officers, declare dividends and recommend fundamental

business changes. The board can delegate but a committee can't amend by-laws or issue shares.

Directors owe a duty of care, which is what an ordinarily prudent person would do. Nonfeasance

(doing nothing) is a breach of the duty of care. Misfeasance is when a director does something

wrong that negatively impacts the corporation. Directors also owe a duty of loyalty, which is to

act in good faith and in the corporation's best interest. Directors also owe the duty of disclosure

and can't usurp an opportunity that the corporation may be interested in without full disclosure

and the approval of the board.

Officers owe the same duties as directors. Officers are corporate agents. (Remember in

Business Associations agency rules and authority). Officers can be removed by the directors.

Officers and directors must be indemnified by the corporation if wholly successful on the merits,

which means found innocent after a trial. The judiciary has the discretion to indemnify regardless

of this rule.

Shareholders may manage the corporation if they have a unanimous shareholder's

agreement, there are 100 or less shareholders, and the shares aren't publicly traded. "Piercing the

corporate veil" is when one commingles corporate and personal funds. This allows a creditor to

go after the corporation itself, either through an individual or a subsidiary. Shareholder

derivative actions are actions taken by shareholders to enforce the rights of the corporation. If the

corporation could or should have brought suit it is a derivative action. In a shareholder derivative action, a shareholder must: have standing (owned the stock at the time the claim arose or acquired it by operation of law, e.g. inheritance); make a demand on the corporation to bring suit; may be liable for expenses if the suit was commenced without reasonable cause; join the corporation as a nominal defendant; and can dismiss or settle only with court approval.

For voting, the record owner of the shares may vote. The record date is when the record owner bought the shares. The record date may not be more than 70 days before a meeting, generally. The record owner's executor may vote his shares upon his death or the record owner may assign a proxy (another person appointed by written authorization). Notice of a meeting to vote should be no fewer than 10 days before the meeting and no more than 60 days before the meeting. A majority of outstanding shares is required (quorum) and is established at the beginning of the meeting. For the election of directors there are three types of voting: plurality; straight; and cumulative. For a plurality, those receiving the top number of votes get elected, unless otherwise specified. For straight voting, a shareholder may vote the total number of shares he owns for each director to be elected if he wishes. For cumulative voting, the shareholder multiplies the number of share he owns by the number of directors to be elected. The shareholder may then vote the total on one director or divide it up amongst several directors.

Shareholders have the right to inspect the books and records, but must have standing and must follow the appropriate procedure. For standing many States have minimum share requirements and also have statutory procedures to be followed.

Distributions are generally in the form of dividends, repurchase or redemptions. Dividends are the most common form of distribution and usually take the form of checks. A repurchase or redemption is a forced sale to a corporation at a price that is set in its articles. For dividends there are two categories: preferred and participating. Preferred means you get paid first, and then the common shareholders split up the balance. Participating means that shareholders are to be paid again. So, if the preferred shares were participating, the preferred shareholders would get their preferred dividends first, and then split, along with the common shareholders, the balance. You will be asked to do math here and you will likely see a question on the bar. A corporation may make a distribution only if it can pass the insolvency and balance sheet tests. The insolvency test means that the corporation will be able to pay its debts as they come due in the normal course of business *after* the dividends are paid. The balance sheet test means that the corporation's total assets will be equal to or greater than its total liabilities *after* the dividend is paid.

Non-profit corporations are formed for a public purpose (benefit) and the purpose must be stated in the articles. A non-profit corporation must have at least three directors usually.

For mergers and share exchanges approval is required by both of the boards of the merging companies and an absolute majority (majority of all shares outstanding) of the shares of both firms. Dissolution may be accomplished through voluntary or involuntary dissolution. Voluntary dissolution requires either: the approval of the board and an absolute majority of the shares, or the written consent of an absolute majority of the shares. Involuntary dissolution is at the discretion of the court and can be accomplished through a shareholder petition or a creditor's petition. Administrative dissolution occurs when the corporation fails to file an annual report.

Corporations that are publicly traded must abide by Federal securities law. The transactions covered under Federal securities law include: misrepresentation (fraud); non-disclosure (insider trading) and tipping (passing insider information for the wrong purpose). The elements of a civil action include a plaintiff (buyer or seller of securities); defendant; materiality; interstate commerce; the action must be within the statute of limitations; and there must be scienter (scienter is a legal term meaning the intent or knowledge of wrongdoing. You'll hear it a lot in law school) or the intent to defraud, not just negligence.

8.3.3 Key Take-Aways

a. Forming a corporation requires articles of incorporation to be filed and organizational meetings to be held.

b. A de jure corporation is formed in accordance with the law and must file an annual report or risk administrative dissolution.

c. A de facto corporation is a good faith attempt to form a corporation and act on the corporation's behalf.

d. When a corporation sells its own shares it is called issuance.

e. Outstanding shares are shares that the corporation has sold but not yet reacquired.

f. Subscriptions are written offers to buy stock that must be accepted by the board.

g. Consideration is what the corporation receives for selling stock and can be tangible or intangible property.

h. Par value is the minimum issuance price, not the fair market value.

i. Watered stock is stock that is sold for less than par value.

j. Treasury stocks are outstanding shares that the corporation has reacquired.

k. Directors are one or more natural persons 18 years or older and are elected by shareholders.

l. A quorum of directors on the board is a majority unless otherwise specified. The minimum is generally one third.

m. Directors set policy, supervise officers, declare dividends, and recommend fundamental business changes.

n. Directors are bound by the same duties as corporate officers.

o. Shareholders may manage a corporation if they have a unanimous shareholder's agreement, there are 100 or less shareholders and the shares aren't publicly traded.

p. Shareholder derivative actions are actions taken by shareholders to enforce the rights of the corporation. A shareholder must have standing, make a demand on the corporation to bring suit, may be liable for expenses if the action is taken without reasonable cause, must join the corporation as a nominal defendant, and can dismiss or settle only with court approval.

q. For voting only the record owner of the shares may vote.

r. Notice of a meeting where voting will occur can be no fewer than 10 days before a meeting.

s. For plurality voting, those receiving the top number of votes get elected.

t. For straight voting, a shareholder may use his total number of shares for each director.

u. For cumulative voting, the shareholder multiples his total number of shares by the total number of directors to be elected.

v. Distributions are usually in the form of dividends, repurchases, or redemptions.

w. Dividends fall into two categories: preferred and participating. Preferred means you get paid first and the difference is split up between the common shareholders. Participating means you get paid preferred first and then get paid again as part of the common shareholder pool.

x. The balance sheet test means the corporation's total assets are equal to or greater than its total liabilities after the dividend is paid.

y. Mergers and acquisitions require approval by the boards of both companies and an absolute majority (majority of shares outstanding) of both firms.

z. Dissolution is either voluntary or involuntary. Involuntary is at the discretion of the court.

aa. Administrative dissolution occurs when a corporation fails to file an annual report.

bb. Federal securities law includes transactions that relate to: misrepresentation (fraud); non-disclosure (insider trading); and tipping (passing insider information).

9. Family Law (State Bar Tested)

9.1 Introduction

Family law is an area decided in state courts, yet there are not many significant distinctions between state law and what you might learn in Family Law class in law school. States generally apply many varieties of factors, and, as a matter of policy, rule out very few factors. Because bar exam essays are supposed to weigh all points of view and arguments, it is possible to write an essay and answer questions based solely off of broad family law points (as a judge in practice likely would consider the same factors), and still receive high marks. We have added a few distinctions, nonetheless.

9.2 Family Law (State Bar Tested)

Premarital agreements are contracts between people who plan to marry. The law doesn't limit the subject matter, but you generally can't include future child support or custody in the agreement. Many States have established Premarital Agreement Acts as a baseline for challenging the validity of a premarital agreement. There are generally three bases for challenging premarital agreements: the agreement wasn't entered into voluntarily; one spouse had a lack of experience or economic sophistication; or there was duress or unconscionability. For a marriage, there must be a license, a ceremony, an officiant, and the parties must exchange promises. The parties must be capable of getting married. Certain capacity issues exist in order for a marriage to be valid. The person must be sane, of proper age, and not be related (incest), which would be grounds for annulment. An officiant can be a member of the clergy, a mayor, the captain of a cruise ship, etc.

Annulment is always based on a ground that predates the marriage. The grounds for annulment are that the marriage is either void or voidable. A void marriage is no marriage at all, such as bigamy, mental incapacity or incest. In other words it wasn't legal in the first place, so it doesn't exist. A voidable marriage is when you are married until you get an annulment. Grounds for a voidable marriage are: fraud; duress; intoxication or temporary insanity; marriage in jest; to permit one party to obtain citizenship; one party is underage (parental consent for ages 16 to 18), or incurable impotence.

Divorce is always handled in a State court and generally at the circuit court level. The State has subject matter jurisdiction when one spouse is domiciled in the State and has been a resident for a certain period of time prior to filing. The residency requirement varies, but a safe range is six months to a year. If any other remedies are required, such as alimony or child support, the State must have personal jurisdiction over the spouse being filed against. Service of process on the other party must always be made. Venue is usually appropriate in any county where the parties reside or the counties where the grounds for divorce arose. The grounds for divorce have morphed over the years. First there had to be fault, like adultery or cruelty. Many States have migrated to no-fault States where the grounds are generally that the marriage is irretrievably broken, or that one spouse is mentally incompetent. For mental incompetence there is generally some time period that the divorcing spouse must wait from the point at which the soon to be divorced spouse was declared mentally incompetent. This can generally be three years, sometimes longer.

Equitable distribution is the doctrine most often used for the distribution of marital property. Many States allow for a partial distribution during divorce proceedings if a spouse is limited in resources. The parties must categorize the assets and then distribute the assets. Separate property is property that is acquired prior to the marriage or received as a gift or inheritance in the sole name of one spouse. Like, Aunt Wilma left a lakeside cabin to her niece

Mary, when Mary was married to Tom. The cabin is Mary's separate property. Everything acquired during marriage is marital property. In the distribution of marital property, a court will consider: the economic circumstances of each party; contributions each spouse made to the marriage (including homemaking); and who was the primary custodian of the children (who generally gets the marital home).

There are many types of alimony, and States vary in what they will allow. Generally there is: pendente lite; bridge-the-gap; rehabilitative; permanent; and durational alimony. A court has the discretion to award pendente lite alimony, which is alimony during the litigation phase of a divorce. Bridge-the-gap alimony eases the transition between married and single life and usually can't exceed two years. Rehabilitative alimony allows a spouse to enhance or acquire training to reenter the job market, if that spouse sacrificed his or her career while the other spouse enhanced their career. Permanent alimony is determined by duration of the marriage. A short duration marriage is less than 7 years, a moderate duration marriage is 7 to 17 years, and a long duration marriage is 17+ years. Durational alimony is alimony that lasts for a specific period of time, but usually can't exceed the length of the marriage. In determining eligibility for alimony a court will look at: the age and physical condition of the spouses; sources of income; educational level; contributions to the marriage; and the standard of living. Alimony may be modified when a significant change in one of the spouse's circumstances occurs such as winning the lottery, getting remarried, or dying.

Custody usually requires the parents to jointly create time-sharing or parenting plan, which includes residential and legal responsibility. Residential responsibility is physical custody. Legal custody is having the right to make legal decisions for the child. Many States require a shared order of responsibility unless it is detrimental to the child, which is the "Best Interests of the Child" doctrine. Remember the "Best Interests of the Child" doctrine. Say it five times out loud. It permeates every facet of family law. To determine custody, courts look at: the parent's physical, mental and emotional fitness; substance abuse; the wishes of the child if they are over the age of 12; whether one parent has a new companion; a history of domestic violence; the ability of the parent to manage the children; and which spouse has better relationships with extended family. Interstate custody battles fall under the Uniform Child Custody and Judicial Enforcement Act (UCCJEA) where the home State of the child is either: the home State of the child; or, the last home State of the child for the past 6 months.

Child support requires the biological parents. If a couple is married and a child is born, the presumption is that the marital father is the father of the child. The obligation for child support continues until the age of 18 and the child has graduated from high school, capped at the age of 19. Child support is most often based on statutory guidelines, but the court can vary the amount of support, based on the earning capacity of the spouses, up or down by five percent. Support can be modified by a change in circumstances, similar to alimony. The Uniform Interstate Family Support Act (UIFSA) operates to erase State boundaries and provides that the original order must be deferred to as long as either the child or one parent continues to live in that forum without modification.

Generally, anyone may be adopted. A married couple, a single adult, a married person acting alone (with the consent of the spouse for a step child), may adopt. For a minor adoptee the consent of both biological parents is required. If parental rights are terminated the parent has no rights. Involuntary termination (ordered by the court) of parental rights happens when children are: abandoned; neglected; abused; or the parent has murdered or committed felony assault of one of their children. The Best Interest of the Child standard permeates and prevails in family law. Hell, you even see it on Law & Order!

9.3 Key Take-Aways

a. For a marriage, there must be a license, a ceremony, an officiant, and the parties must exchange promises.

b. In order for the marriage to be valid each party must be: sane; of proper age; and not related.

c. A void marriage is a marriage that wasn't legal in the first place.

d. A voidable marriage is based on: fraud; duress; intoxication or temporary insanity; it was in jest; it was done to obtain citizenship; a party is underage; or impotence.

e. Divorce is a State action and generally handled at the circuit level.

f. If remedies other than divorce are required, the State must have personal jurisdiction over the spouse being filed against.

g. Venue for divorce is any county where the parties reside or where the grounds for divorce arose.

h. Georgia recognizes equitable distribution for distributing marital property.

i. Separate property is property acquired by a spouse prior to the marriage or received as a gift or inheritance in the sole name of one of the spouses.

j. Courts consider: economic circumstances; contributions to the marriage (homemaking included) and the primary custodian of the children, when determining equitable distribution.

k. The types of alimony are: pendent lite; bridge-the-gap; rehabilitative; permanent; and durational.

l.   In determining alimony courts look at: age and physical condition of the spouses; sources of income; educational level; contributions to the marriage; and standard of living.

m.   Custody requires parents to create a parenting plan, which advocates the BEST INTERESTS of THE CHILD.

n.   To determine custody courts look at: the parent's physical, mental and emotional fitness; substance abuse; the wishes of the child (over 12); if a parent has a new companion; a history of domestic violence; a parent's ability to manage the children; and the spouse's relationships with extended family.

o.   The home State of the child is either: the home State of the child; or the home State of the child for the past six months.

p.   The obligation for child support continues until the age of 18 and the child has graduated from high school, capped at the age of 19.

q.   Child support is based on statutory guidelines, but the court can vary by five percent (up or down).

r.   Involuntary termination of parental rights occurs when: children are abandoned, neglected, or abused; or a parent has murdered one of their children.

9.4 Introduction to Delinquency and Dependency

Georgia enacted a new juvenile code (NJC) in January of 2014 which includes a new focus on: the enhanced presence of lawyers in delinquency proceedings; new guidelines for dependency proceedings; a new approach for the termination of parental rights; and a new category of youth called Children in Need of Services (CHINS). The Division of Family and Child Services (DFCS) works in concert with the juvenile courts to ensure that aspects of delinquency and dependency are administered properly.

In many instances, issues regarding delinquency and dependency are addressed as functions of family law and may be included in family law essays on the bar examination, while not called out separately as a tested bar exam topic. As such, we have included a general overview of delinquency and dependency along with a "Take-away" section, which highlights the changes in the law due to new legislation.

9.5 Delinquency

Juvenile justice is doled out by a State's juvenile justice system which has a primary purpose of rehabilitation. Delinquency is addressed in Article 6 of the NJC. Delinquent acts are not considered crimes because they are committed by children. Juveniles have most of the same rights as adults, except they traditionally have no right to bail or a jury trial. Generally children under the age of 18 are first referred to juvenile court, which retains jurisdiction over a case until the child turns 19. The players in a juvenile case are the State attorney (prosecution), the counsel for the child, the Juvenile courts, and the Division of Family and Children Services (DFCS).

Juvenile courts use the term "taken into custody" instead of arrested. Generally a child must be released from custody as soon as reasonably possible to a responsible party who must make a written report or sign a probable cause affidavit. The State may decide to keep a child from going through formal court proceedings by issuing a civil citation, which refers the child for community service or intervention services. Generally, a child must appear before a judge at a detention hearing within 24 hours of being taken into custody and can't be detained for more than 21 days before trial. Also, generally a child can't be held for more than 15 days before being found delinquent at which point the child is moved to a treatment center. At the detention hearing the judge determines if there is probable cause and if detention is necessary. A judge may decide to order non-secure detention (custody of a parent) or secure detention (juvenile facility). A child may be transferred to adult court by waiver (a judge decides), indictment (by a grand jury), or information (prosecutor decides). Generally a prosecutor transfers by information (a direct file) if the child is between the ages of 14 and 17 and his offense was violent, he has repeated violent offenses, or is a danger to the community. Delinquency charges are served on a child by summons and arraignments must be held within 48 hours of filing a delinquency petition if the child is detained. Regarding pleas, the court must: advise the child that he has a right to counsel before making a plea; determine if there is a factual basis for the delinquent act; make sure that the child knowingly and intelligently waived his rights; make sure that the plea is voluntary; and ensure that the child is aware of the consequences of his plea. A child has a constitutional right to a trial (not a jury trial), may demand discovery, and charges must be proven beyond a reasonable doubt.

The types of facilities a child may be sentenced to are: minimum-risk nonresidential (day treatment five days a week with unsupervised community access); non-secure residential (residential program with overnight stays and supervised community access); high-risk residential (structured residential, strict schedule and up to 72 hours of supervised community access); and maximum-risk residential (maximum security residential, no community access).

If a child is convicted of an offense punishable by death or life imprisonment he is sentenced as an adult and can appeal the order to a court of appeals.

9.6 Dependency

Dependency is the term used to protect children from abuse, abandonment or neglect, meaning that the child is dependent on the State. Article 3 of the NJC governs dependency proceedings. Parents have a right to an attorney, notice of all hearings, and visitation rights, unless the court specifies otherwise. The State usually uses reasonable efforts to keep the child in the home with services, or if the child is removed, uses reasonable efforts to reunite the child with his family as soon as possible. The three main goals of most States regarding a dependency program are safety, stability and welfare. The parties involved are: the parents (each is a separate party); a guardian ad litem for the child; and the respective State department dealing with dependency issues. In the cases of a child who: is placed in a skilled nursing facility; prescribed psychotropic medication; has a developmental disability; or who is a victim of human trafficking, an attorney must be appointed for the child. Dependency cases are usually heard in juvenile court. The juvenile court has jurisdiction until the child turns 18 (which can be extended to 21 or 22 if an immigration case is involved).

The stages of a dependency case are: shelter (if emergency removal is required); arraignment; adjudication (trial); disposition; judicial review; and permanency. Based on the State's civil and administrative procedure there are specific deadlines (number of days) in which these stages must be accomplished. These are State specific.

People who must report abuse or neglect are: doctors and nurses; mental health professionals; teachers and school administrators; social, day care and other child care workers; law enforcement; judges; and college or university administrators. If not they may face criminal charges. Confidentiality does not apply to reporting abuse or neglect. A person can't use privilege to avoid testifying about abuse or neglect. Privilege does apply to attorneys and clergy.

Once a report is made an investigation must occur generally within 60 days and includes interviews with the family and home visits. Sometimes a specialized child protection team will be involved. During the investigation the respective State department may close the case if there is no basis, remove the child to a shelter, or decide not to remove the child and open a case. The removal of a child must be based on probable cause of abuse, neglect or abandonment. Shelter hearings are held generally within 24 hours of a child's removal and the parents must be given

notice. Sometimes a court will, instead of removal, order an after school program, child care,

education or domestic violence counseling. If the child is removed the place they live

temporarily is called placement. Options for placement include: living with the other parent; a

relative; a friend of the family or person close to the child (court approved); or a foster home.

Dependency petitions must be filed generally with 21 days after the shelter hearing and a

diligence search must be performed to ensure that the parents are given notice. Arraignments are

generally held within 28 days of the shelter hearing. An adjudicatory hearing is conducted by a

judge and dependency must be proven by a preponderance of the evidence. The grounds are

abuse, neglect or abandonment. The State department develops a case plan to fix the problem,

where all players are in attendance. The parents may be provided education and health services,

they may be evaluated, or get counseling. Permanency goals are the end goals for the child.

Permanency options are: reunification with the parents; adoption; permanent guardianship;

permanent placement with a fit relative; or placement in another permanent living arrangement,

generally using this order of priority.

Judicial review hearings are held to monitor the progress of the child. The first review is

usually held no more than 90 days after disposition and then once every six months. The judge

looks at: whether the State department has made reasonable efforts to achieve its goals; whether

the parents have substantially complied with the case plan; whether the child is in an appropriate

placement; whether the plan goals should be changed; and if additional services are required.

Termination of parental rights requires notice of an advisory hearing and is addressed in

Article 4 of the NJC. Failure to appear serves as consent. Personal service on the parents is

required. If the child has been out of the home for 12 to 22 months the State department must file a petition to terminate parental rights. Grounds for terminating parental rights include: a parent voluntarily surrendering rights; abandonment of the child; parental conduct poses a threat to the child; the parents haven't complied with the case plan; the parents are incarcerated; the parents have subjected the child to sexual battery or abuse; the parents have been murdered; or the parents have histories of alcohol or substance abuse. The standard of proof for terminating parental rights is clear and convincing. So far in our discussions, we've discussed the burden of proof as being a preponderance of the evidence or clear and convincing evidence. For clarification, a preponderance of the evidence is who has the most evidence. Like if you stack it up, which stack is the highest? Clear and convincing evidence is a higher standard. It doesn't deal with the quantity of evidence; it deals with the quality of evidence. If you look at the evidence and there is only one conclusion, it's generally clear and convincing.

9.7 Delinquency and Dependency Key Take-Aways

a. Article 6 of the NJC focuses upon the increased presence of attorneys for parties in the juvenile delinquency process. The NJC mandates that any allegations regarding delinquency must be in a petition that is filed by an attorney. This mandate was enacted to take the burden away from the police and probation officers who previously were responsible for filing documents alleging delinquency. The NJC also mandates that prosecuting attorneys conduct delinquency proceedings on the state's behalf. The NJC also reserves the right of waiver of counsel to the child, not parental or other representation.

b. Article 3 of the NJC, governing dependency proceedings, enhances the purpose of dependency proceedings by: assisting and protecting rights of children during proceedings; expediting dependency proceedings; providing prompt and optimum protection for children; and assuring that the best interests of the child, to include health and safety, are a priority in dependency proceedings. The NJC also expanded the definition of a child to include anyone under the age of 18; or anyone under the care of DFCS aged 22 years or less; or anyone at the age of 23, under the care of DFCS who may be eligible for independent living services. The NJC mandates that both an attorney and a guardian ad litem (GAL) be appointed for a dependent child and in some instances the attorney may serve as the GAL unless a conflict arises. The NJC also mandates that the first review hearing be held prior to 75 days elapsing from the date of the child's removal and each four months from that point.

c. Article 4 of the NJC governs the termination of parental rights by specifically: protecting a dependent child from parents who cannot provide for the child's safety and care; expediting wait time for a dependent child's parents to rectify issues that prevent the child from returning to his or her home; assuring that the physical, mental and emotional needs of the child are the primary emphasis during proceedings; protecting the constitutional rights of all parties during proceedings; and ensuring stability in the child's life. The NJC affords a child who has not been adopted in three years to petition for the reinstatement of parental rights, which had been previously terminated. Article 4's mantra is the best interest of the child.

d. Article 5 of the NJC addresses CHINS, which is an attempt to differentiate between immature behavior exhibited at home or school, from delinquent behavior. If a complaint is filed alleging that a child is in fact a CHINS child, the child can be held for no more than 24 hours before a probable cause hearing. Once probable cause has been determined a child may be detained an additional 72 hours (excluding weekends and holidays) to locate appropriate placement. If detained, an adjudication hearing must be held within 10 days of adjudication. If a child is found to be a CHINS child a disposition must be held within 60 days of adjudication. Once a CHINS order has been decreed violations require reasonable doubt as the standard of proof.

10. Trusts, Wills, and Estates (State Bar Tested)

10.1 Introduction

The key concepts addressed in this section are categorized under wills and trusts. Estates float back and forth between the two. The key concepts for wills includes: probate and freedom of disposition, intestacy; per stirpes distribution; the formalities and functions of a will; capacity issues and tests; and will construction. The key concepts for trusts are: the creation of trusts; types of trusts, e.g. revocable trusts; other will substitutes; limits on disposition; fiduciary administration; trust modification; and powers of appointment.

10.2 Trusts, Wills, and Estates

Georgia's relevant law is called the Revised Probate Code of 1998. Probate property (property left by a decedent) passes by will or intestacy. Non-probate property may be transferred by will substitutes, such as an inter vivos (between the living) trust, or a life insurance policy. A person can devise real property and bequeath personal property. The Uniform Probate Code (UPC) governs probate actions. The three functions of probate are: (1) to provide evidence of transfer of title; (2) to protect creditors; and (3) to distribute the decedent's property. Intestate means there was no will. Any part of an estate that is not disposed of by will passes by intestate succession to the decedent's heirs. The intestate share of a decedent's surviving spouse is the entire estate, if no descendant or parent survives. If there is no taker, the intestate estate passes to the State.

States use three methods of distribution for an intestate estate: English per stirpes (strict); modern per stirpes; and per capita at each generation. Per stirpes literally means, "by the stocks". English per stirpes, which Georgia follows, treats each line of descent equally, divided into as many shares as there are living children and deceased children, who have descendants.

Everybody gets a trophy! Modern per stirpes is the same as English per stirpes if there are living children. If there are no living children, then the estate is divided equally at the first generation where there are living takers. Per capita by each generation distributes the initial division of shares to the closest generation with live descendants, then the deceased on that same level are treated as one pot, dropped down and divided amongst descendants. Per stirpes is a difficult concept. There were a few questions on my final and maybe one or two on the State bar exam. I didn't spend much time on it. I figured if I only missed those few questions, I would be good. Anything that rhymes with herpes can't be good! In order to disinherit someone you must make an affirmative statement in the will. "I don't want anything to go to my nephew Joe." An advancement is a gift given during the lifetime of a decedent instead of waiting until the will is executed. A constructive trust is not a trust; it is a remedy to make sure property is conveyed to the rightful claimant.

The core formalities of a will are writing, signature, and attestation (witnesses). The functions of these formalities are evidentiary, ritual and protective and channeling, respectively. Georgia requires that a will must be witnessed by at least two subscribing (sign at the bottom) witnesses who are present when the testator signs. The testator must sign in the presence of the witnesses. In Georgia, a testator and witness may be age 14 or more. A witness who is a beneficiary (gets something) can sign, but loses his share (this is called purging). The Wills Act states that a will must be authentic, must be voluntary, must have been meant to be a will (testamentary intent), and must follow the formalities. Generally wills must comply with the formalities and requirements of the Wills Act, if not the will is denied probate. Courts may allow a will into probate that substantially complies with the requirements and formalities. The Harmless Error Rule states that a court may excuse non-compliance if there is clear and convincing evidence showing the testamentary intent. A will may be revoked by a subsequent writing or by a revocatory act like, destroying it. A holographic will is written by the testator's hand (handwritten) and signed by the testator. Attesting witnesses are not required. Georgia does not recognize holographic wills.

There is a concept called dependent relative revocation. It means that if a testator relied on a new will being valid and destroyed the old will, but the new will was invalid, the court will probate the old will if it can be found. There is another concept called revival of a revoked will. This means that if a testator executes one will and subsequently develops a second will, and subsequently revokes the second will, then the first will is revived. All papers present at the time of execution that are intended to be part of a will are considered to be integrated into the will. Being referenced in the will is known as incorporation by reference.

Capacity is a key factor in challenging a will. There are a few tests and doctrines. The Cunningham Test requires that the: testator understands the nature of his actions; he knows the extent of his property; he understands the disposition; he knows the natural objects of his bounty; and that the will represents his wishes. The Insane Delusions Test requires that in order to prove a lack of capacity, insane delusions must materially affect the disposition of the will. The Undue Influence Doctrine states that evidence must show: that the donor was susceptible; the wrongdoer had the opportunity; the wrongdoer had the disposition; and the result appeared to be undue influence.

Courts always start with a presumption to avoid intestacy, meaning they look for ways to validate a will. A court can reform (rewrite or substitute terms) the terms of a will if clear and convincing evidence is available to show the testator's intent. There is a rule (don't laugh) called the No Residue of a Residue Rule, which basically means that if people are left something in a will and it doesn't get distributed, then any residue will be distributed through intestate succession. Apparently the courts don't like residues. If a devisee (person who is supposed to get something) does not survive the testator, the devise lapses. The devisee must survive the testator, unless the testator specifies otherwise. Most States have created antilapse statutes, which allow for the substitution of another beneficiary for the devisee who died (predeceased devisee). The presumed intent of antilapse statutes is that the courts presume the testator would like to substitute the gift to the devisee's descendants rather than it passing under the common law of lapse, which may result in the gift going to someone the testator doesn't like.

Ademption applies to specific devises. "I want my 1932 Hudson to go to my niece Beverly." There are two theories relating to ademption. The identity theory states that if the specific devise (the 1932 Hudson) doesn't exist, the gift is extinguished. Under the intent theory, cash can be used as a replacement for the missing devise. Abatement is a reduction in distribution when the estate doesn't have enough assets to cover all of the distribution.

There are certain limits on disposition. If a testator's spouse married him after his will was executed, as the surviving spouse she is entitled to receive no less than her intestate share, which is usually one-half of the estate. If a testator omits a child after the execution of a will, the omitted child receives the same amount living children would equal to their intestate share.

A trust is the legal title of property held by one party for the benefit of another. Trustees have legal title, beneficiaries have equitable title. The Uniform Trust Code (UTC) governs trusts. A valid trust requires: intent; purpose; res (trust property, e.g. cash, land, etc.); a trustee; and ascertainable (you can identify them) beneficiaries. If the res in a trust includes real property the SOF applies, and usually applies to testamentary trusts and wills. Generally the persons who create a trust are called: settlor, grantor, or trustor.

There are different types of trusts. An express trust exhibits the express intent of the settlor. For a private trust there must be ascertainable beneficiaries. For a charitable trust it must: benefit the public, be liberally construed, and can have indefinite (not identified right now) beneficiaries. A trust is generally revocable, unless it states that it is irrevocable. The Cy Pres Doctrine applies to the substitution of another beneficiary of a charitable trust if the original beneficiary ceases to exist, and is enforced by the attorney general of each State. A resulting trust is when an express trust fails and assets remain, without any alternative disposition being specified, and the court steps in to identify an alternative. A constructive trust is an equitable remedy, not a trust. We talked about that earlier.

A settlor can: revoke a trust; appoint income; add or withdraw property; remove trustees; receive income; and act as the sole trustee. A beneficiary can: disclaim interest; sue to compel; remove a trustee for breach of trust; obtain an accounting; and freely transfer interest. A trustee's duties include: segregation of assets; accounting; he must perform personally, he can delegate investment functions if he doesn't have the expertise; he can diversify; and he must be fair and impartial. More generally, a trustee's functions are: custodial, administrative, investment, and distribution.

The Prudent Trustee Rule states that: a trustee must observe statutes; he must take into account probable income; and he must act to protect the safety and preservation of the principal of the trust. A trustee can't engage in self-dealing. If he does, his only defenses are consent or ratification. Consent means he did it with the consent of a beneficiary. Ratification means he did it with the consent of all of the beneficiaries, in writing. We discussed ratification with regard to shareholders. A trustee can be removed for: breach of trust; incapacity; unfitness; refusal to account; or conflict of interest.

If there is fraud a creditor can reach the principal of a trust, otherwise it can reach only what the settlor receives in income. Generally, creditors can reach a beneficiary's interest. Spendthrift Trusts were created to prohibit the transfer of a beneficiary's interest before it is paid to him. This was intended to be sort of an allowance for a beneficiary who would probably piss away the entire principal of the trust if he could get his hands on it. Exceptions to this are alimony and child support.

10.3 Key Take-Aways

a. Probate property passes by will or intestacy.

b. Non-probate property can be transferred by will substitutes, such as a life insurance policy.

c. The three functions of probate are: to provide evidence of transfer of title; to protect creditors; and to distribute the decedent's property.

d. The three methods for distribution of an intestate estate are: English per stirpes; modern per stirpes and per capita at each generation. Georgia follows English (strict) per stirpes.

e. An advancement is a gift given during the lifetime of the decedent instead of waiting until the will is executed.

f. A constructive trust is an equitable remedy, not a trust.

g. The core formalities of a will are: writing; signature; and attestation.

h. The functions of the formalities are: evidentiary; ritual and protective; and channeling.

i. Witnesses must be present for attestation purposes.

j. Witnesses must be age 14 or more.

k. The Wills Act requires that a will be: authentic; voluntary; intended to be a will; cognizant of the formalities.

l. The Harmless Error Rule allows a court to excuse non-compliance with the formalities if there is clear and convincing evidence of testamentary intent.

m. Dependent relative revocation is a concept that allows a court to probate an original will, when a testator relied on a new will which was invalid and he destroyed the old will. The old will must be found in order for this to occur.

n. Revival of a revoked will occurs when a testator executes one will and subsequently develops a second will and later revokes it. In this case the first will is revived.

o. If a document is referenced in a will it is said to be incorporated by reference.

p. The Cunningham Test requires that the: testator understands the nature of his actions; knows the extent of his property; understands the disposition; knows the natural objects of his bounty; and the will represents his wishes.

q. The Insane Delusions Test requires that in order to prove a lack of capacity, insane delusions must materially affect the disposition of the will.

r. The Undue Influence Doctrine states that evidence must show: the donor was susceptible; the wrongdoer had the opportunity and the disposition; and the result appeared to be undue influence.

s. The No Residue of a Residue Rule operates to distribute any residue that doesn't get distributed through probate, by intestate succession.

t. If a devisee doesn't survive the testator, the devise lapses.

u. Antilapse statutes allow for the substitution of another beneficiary when the original beneficiary doesn't survive the testator.

v. Ademption applies to specific devises. If the devise doesn't exist, the gift is extinguished.

w. Abatement is a reduction in distribution when the estate doesn't have the assets to cover distribution.

x. A spouse's intestate share is usually one-half of the estate.

y. A trust is the legal title of property held by one party for the benefit of another.

z. A valid trust requires: intent; purpose; res; a trustee; and ascertainable beneficiaries.

aa. An express trust exhibits the express intent of the settlor.

bb. A private trust must have ascertainable beneficiaries.

cc. A charitable trust must: benefit the public; be liberally construed; and can have indefinite beneficiaries.

dd. A trust is revocable, unless it states that it is irrevocable.

ee. The Cy Pres Doctrine allows the court to substitute a beneficiary of a charitable trust if the original beneficiary ceases to exist, and is enforced by the attorney general.

ff. A resulting trust is when an express trust fails and assets remain, without an alternative disposition being made. The court may identify an alternative.

gg. A settlor can: revoke a trust; appoint income; add or withdraw property; remove trustees; receive income; and act as sole trustee.

hh. A beneficiary can: disclaim interest; sue to compel; remove a trustee for breach of trust; obtain an accounting; and freely transfer interest.

ii. A trustee's duties are: segregation of assets; accounting; he must perform personally; he can delegate investment functions; he can diversify; and he must be fair and impartial.

jj. A trustee's functions are categorized as: custodial; administrative; investment; and distribution.

kk. The Prudent Trustee Rule states that: a trustee must observe statutes; he must take into account probable income; he must act to protect the safety and preservation of the principal of the trust; and he can't engage in self-dealing.

ll. A trustee can be removed for: breach of trust; incapacity; unfitness; refusal to account; or conflict of interest.

mm. If fraud exists a creditor can reach the principal of a trust, otherwise it can reach only what the settlor receives in income.

nn. A Spendthrift Trust prohibits the transfer of a beneficiary's interest before it is paid. Exceptions are alimony and child support.

11. Non-Monetary Remedies (State Bar Tested)

11.1 Introduction

Non-Monetary Remedies ("NMR"), sometimes called Equity or Equitable Remedies, is an area of law peppered into doctrinal essay questions. Approach NMR in the same manner as you would Ethics (see Chapter 12) because you are likely not to receive a question based solely on this subject. More often than not, bar examiners will be explicit in whether you should address remedies. Pay attention to the call of the question. If you are instructed not to write about NMR (or, alternatively, to write only about something other than NMR), then any time spent discussing NMR is wasted and you will not receive any points (even if your argument is valid). Other times the question will be less explicit, and, where appropriate, including a small paragraph (or even a sentence or two) in your analysis about the appropriate remedy may garner you a few extra points.

11.2 Things to Know

REMEDIES			
Equitable		**Legal**	
Restitution	Promissory Estoppel	Expectation Damages	Actual Damages
Reformation	Reliance Damages	Compensatory Damages	Consequential Damages
Rescission	Expectation Damages	Specific Performance	Incidental Damages

In Georgia, equity is within the jurisdiction of the superior courts of each county and must be a part of the pleadings, sustained by sufficient evidence. Equitable remedies are appropriate when the legal remedy is inadequate and are feasible when both the person ordered to act and the property are within the forum. One of the following must occur: (1) the subject matter must be unique or rare; (2) damages are speculative or uncertain; (3) multiple suits would be required; (4) insolvency of defendant makes judgment uncollectable; or (5) irreparable harm would result from the defendant's conduct that could not be fully compensated by money judgment.

Relief: Injunctions require a party to do something ("mandatory") or refrain from doing something ("prohibitive"). You will likely see them in a tort or contract question. Injunctive relief is when: (1) the legal remedy is inadequate; (2) an injunction is feasible; (3) hardship to the defendant does not outweigh benefit to plaintiff; and (4) no defenses. Injunctions are *normally* available for: (1) continuous trespass to land; (2) conversion of unique chattel; and (3) to prevent the continuation of a wrongfully instated lawsuit, and *sometimes* available: (1) to eliminate nuisance; (2) prevent waste; or (3) tortuous interference (which requires a valid contract, scienter, intentional interference, and damages). Injunctive relief is *not normally* available for defamation, trade libel, or publication of private facts about the plaintiff.

Temporary injunctive relief is provided with notice to the adverse party or, without notice, with a temporary restraining order. For temporary injunctive relief there must be irreparable harm and a likelihood of success.

Mandatory relief may be declined if an act: (1) requires the application of taste; (2) requires special skills or is complex in nature; (3) is beyond the ability of the defendant to perform; or (4) entails personal services.

Contempt: Civil contempt may be instituted by a private party to compensate the plaintiff for damages caused by the defendant's disobedience or to compel defendant's compliance. Criminal contempt is direct if in the presence of court or indirect when outside the presence of court and based upon willful disregard of a court order.

Specific Performance: Equity requires a contract to be specific in terms of identity of parties, price, time and manner of payment, and description of subject matter. Elements of specific performance include: (1) a valid contract; (2) all conditions have been met; and (3) mutuality of remedies. In Georgia, inadequacy of price, while not alone sufficient to rescind a contract, may justify a court in refusing to decree specific performance.

Time of Essence Clause: Courts may decline to enforce such a clause if: (1) tardiness is slight; (2) loss to other party is slight; or (3) undue hardship to the forfeiting party. Generally, equity will seek a waiver of this clause.

Non-Compete Covenant: Courts may grant this covenant if: (1) reasonable as activity prohibited; (2) the geographic area is limited; or (3) duration of time is not unduly burdensome.

Restitution is usually provided in equity by a constructive trust or equitable lien.

Equitable Defenses include unclean hands, laches, arbitrary time bar, hardship, impossibility, and free speech.

11.3 Key Take-Aways

a. Non-monetary remedies (equitable remedies) are for when legal remedy is inadequate.

b. Both the person ordered to act and the object of property must be within the forum.

c. Pay attention to the requirements for equitable remedy. (One on five must occur).

d. Know when injunctions are and aren't normally available.

e. Injunctions can be mandatory or prohibitive.

f. Contempt can be civil (to compensate for damages) or criminal (direct if in presence of court, or indirect when outside court, but based upon willful disregard of court order).

g. Specific performance requires a valid contract, all conditions have been met, and mutuality of remedies.

12. Professional Responsibilities (Ethics) (MPRE and State Bar Tested)

12.1 Introduction

The Professional responsibilities course, or ethics as we call it, is all about how an attorney should act in different situations as governed by the Model Rules of Professional Conduct (MRPC). Professional responsibilities as a subject, is tested in two forums. The first forum is the MPRE. The second forum is in the essay portion of the State section of the Georgia bar examination. The State bar examinations usually will provide an essay question that will have to do with property, criminal procedure, or one of the other Federal legal subjects, and in the last paragraph, a question regarding professional responsibilities will be thrown in. For example, a person contracted to buy property from another person, and the other person had already conveyed the property to someone else, but the person he conveyed it to failed to record the deed. The person contracting to buy the property comes to you as an attorney asking you for advice. The attorney usually knows something and either doesn't disclose, or is asked to do something outside of ethical bounds. You will need a good understanding to respond to the question regarding the attorney's ethical dilemma and the rules associated with the proper course of action. Again, it is *always* tested on the State bar examination essay component.

The key concepts included in professional responsibilities are: the client-lawyer relationship; the attorney's role as counselor; the attorney's role as advocate; transaction with person other than clients; dealing with law firm and associates; public service; information about legal services; maintaining the integrity of the profession; and judicial ethics.

12.2 Professional Responsibilities

While taking this class (not unlike studying for the bar examinations) we struggled with the amount of information. When we asked for guidance we were just given more information.

This did not help. So, we created a plan of attack by reducing the Model Rules of Professional Conduct (MRPC) to a few pages, grouped by: key concept; rule number; subject; and a short description of the rule. A person can remember a few pages, not six-hundred. It may be found in Exhibit 4 of this book. It also contains the American Bar Association's Model Code of Judicial Administration.

12.3 Key Take-Aways

Consult Exhibit 4 in the back of this book. The topics tested on the MPRE and the State bar examination change frequently so it is best to have an understanding of the rules so that when you are given a fact scenario you can do your best to apply the rule. Remember, in essays the professional responsibilities component is almost always tacked on to the bottom of a fact scenario that deals with something else, like property or criminal procedure. Issues of reasonable fee arrangements and conflicts of interest come up regularly.

Conclusion

It is our sincere hope that this book is helpful in reducing the volume of information in order to afford students more time toward study in not having to filter through the mass of information that will be provided to them by their schools and commercial bar prep programs.

During our bar prep course equal weight was given to each topic. We feel that this is not an accurate portrayal of the topics. You can see it in the difference in size between *Law School "In-Brief"* and this book, which is one-third the size. Remember to look at the NCBE outlines which are online. They are helpful in understanding which sub-topics are most important. Use this as a guide in determining which areas to focus more attention. If you take a practice exam and get only 50% correct, don't be discouraged. The practice exam will almost certainly not have the same balance among the various sub-topics as the Georgia bar exam. So if, in your score of 50%, you see that you were correct in all of your negligence torts questions, but struggled with conversion, you are doing better on questions more likely to be tested on the Bar (negligence) than those which will be sprinkled in (intentional torts).

It is our belief that if you follow the strategy in *Law School "In-Brief"* and commit the topics to memory, your probability of success will be high.

References

1. Property Law: Rules, Policies and Practices; Singer, Fifth Edition, Aspen Publishers, 2010. Also Barbri property lecture and GA Code Title 44 (2015).

2. Constitutional Law: A Contemporary Approach; Maggs and Smith; Second Edition, West, 2011. Also, Barbri constitutional law lecture.

3. The Georgia State Constitution; Hill, Oxford University Press, 2011.

4. State Constitutions of the United States, Maddex, Second Edition, CQ Press, 2006.

5. Civil Procedure: Cases and Materials; Friedenthal, Miller, Sexton and Hershkoff, Eleventh Edition, West American Casebook Series, 2013. Also, Barbri civil procedure lecture.

6. 2013-2014 Civil Procedure Supplement; Friedenthal, Miller, Sexton and Hershkoff, West American Casebook Series, 2013.

7. Criminal Law: A Contemporary Approach; Cases, Statutes, and Problems; Bloch and McMunigal, Aspen Publishers, 2005. Also, Barbri criminal law lecture.

8. Georgia Court Rules and Procedure: Volume I – State, Thomson Reuters (2016).

9. Understanding Criminal Law; Joshua Dressler; Sixth Edition, LexisNexis, 2012.

10. Criminal Procedure Investigation; Chemerinsky and Levenson; Second Edition; Aspen Casebook Series, 2013. Also Barbri criminal procedures lecture and The Criminal Code of Georgia (2015).

11. Problems in Contract Law: Cases and Materials, Knapp, Crystal and Prince, Seventh Edition, Aspen Casebook Series, 2012. Also, Barbri contracts lecture.

12. Georgia Contracts: Law and Litigations; Second Edition, Thomson Reuters, 2011.

13. Commercial Paper: Personal Notes from Barbri lecture on Commercial Paper, also GA Code Title 11 Art. 3 "Uniform Commercial Code – Negotiable Instruments".

14. Secured Transactions: Personal Notes from Barbri lecture on Secured Transactions, also GA Code Title 11 Art. 9 "Uniform Commercial Code – Secured Transactions".

15. Torts and Compensation: Personal Accountability and Social Responsibility for Injury, Dobbs, Hayden and Bublick, Seventh Edition, West American Casebook Series, 2103. Also, Barbri torts lecture and GA Code Title 51 (2015).

16. Evidence: Fisher, Third Edition, Foundation Press, 2013. Also, Barbri evidence lecture.

17. Evidence: Federal Rules of Evidence; 2013-2014 Statutory & Case Supplement, Fisher, Third Edition, Foundation Press, 2013.

18. Courtroom Handbook on Georgia Evidence; Milich, 2016 Edition, Thomson Reuters, 2016.

19. Business Associations: Cases and Materials on Agency, Partnerships, and Corporations; Klein, Ramseyer and Bainbridge, Eighth Edition, Foundation Press, 2012.

20. Partnerships: Personal Notes from Barbri Lecture on General Partnerships.

21. Corporations: GA Code Title 14 (2015).

22. Contemporary Family Law, Abrahams, Cahn, Ross and Meyer, Third Edition, American Casebook Series, 2012. Also, Barbri family law lecture and GA Code Title 19 (2015).

23. Wills, Trusts, and Estates, Dukeminier and Sitkoff, Ninth Edition, Aspen Casebook Series, 2013. Also, Barbri trust and wills lectures and Revised Probate Code of 1998.

24. Equity: GA Code Title 13 (2015).

25. 2014 Selected Standards on Professional Responsibility, Morgan and Rotunda, Foundation Press, 2014.

26. Georgia Bar Journal, "Georgia's Juvenile Code: New Law for the New Year, A Collaborative Article," December 2013, pages 13-19.

Exhibits

Exhibit 1: Rule Against Perpetuities Chart
(See p. 16)

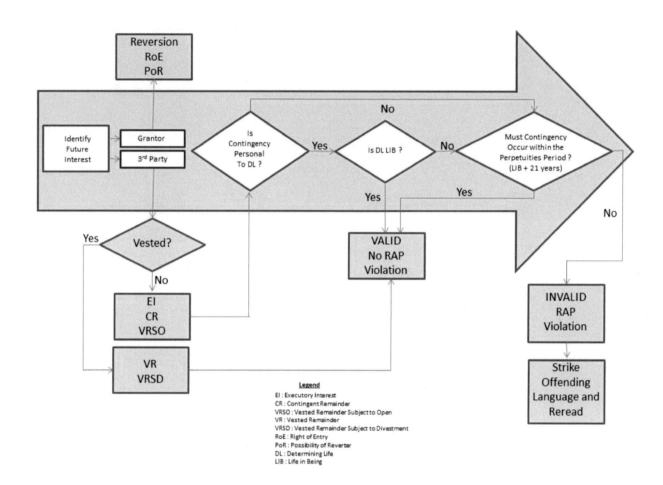

Legend

EI : Executory Interest
CR : Contingent Remainder
VRSO : Vested Remainder Subject to Open
VR : Vested Remainder
VRSD : Vested Remainder Subject to Divestment
RoE : Right of Entry
PoR : Possibility of Reverter
DL : Determining Life
LIB : Life in Being

Exhibit 2: United States Constitution Quick Reference

Note: Italicized areas are most significant for legal study and exam preparation.

Abbreviations: Art. = Article; § = Section; Cl. = Clause

ARTICLES

Art. 1

§ 1   All legislative powers are vested in Congress; a Senate and House of Representatives

§ 2

Cl. 1	House elected by the people of the United States
Cl. 2	Qualification of representatives in the House
Cl. 3	Appointment of representatives and direct taxes
Cl. 4	Vacancies
Cl. 5	*Officers and Impeachment; House has the sole power of impeachment*

§ 3

Cl. 1	Senate Composition
Cl. 2	Classification of Senators
Cl. 3	Qualification of Senators
Cl. 4	President of the Senate
Cl. 5	Officers of the Senate
Cl. 6	*Trial of impeachment; Senate has the sole power to try impeachments*
Cl. 7	*Judgment in cases of impeachment; removal, disqualification and subject to Indictment*

§ 4

Cl. 1	Elections; Senators and Representatives
Cl. 2	Meetings of Congress

§ 5

Cl. 1	Organization of Congress
Cl. 2	Rules of proceedings; punishment of members
Cl. 3	Journal of proceedings
Cl. 4	Adjournment

§ 6

Cl. 1	Compensation and privileges of members
Cl. 2	Holding other offices

§ 7

Cl. 1	Bills and resolutions; revenue bills
Cl. 2	*Approval or veto of bills; passage over veto; (Presentment Clause)*

Cl. 3   Approval or veto of resolutions, orders or votes; passage over veto

§ 8

Cl. 1   *Powers of Congress; taxation*

Cl. 2   *Power of Congress to borrow money*

Cl. 3   *Power of congress to regulate commerce*

Cl. 4   Naturalization; bankruptcy

Cl. 5   Coinage, weights and measures

Cl. 6   Counterfeiting

Cl. 7   Post office and post roads

Cl. 8   *Patents and copyrights*

Cl. 9   *Inferior tribunals; inferior to the supreme Court*

Cl. 10   Offenses; Piracies and Felonies on the high seas; offenses against the Law of Nations

Cl. 11   *Declare War*

Cl. 12   *Raise and support armies*

Cl. 13   Navy

Cl. 14   Government and regulation of land and naval forces

Cl. 15   Calling forth militia

Cl. 16   Organizing militia

Cl. 17   Authority over places purchased or ceded

Cl. 18   *All necessary and proper laws (Necessary and Proper Clause)*

§ 9

Cl. 1   Prohibited powers; migration or importation of persons

Cl. 2   *Habeus Corpus*

Cl. 3   *Bill of Attainder; ex post facto laws*

Cl. 4   Capitation of direct taxes

Cl. 5   Tax on exports from State

Cl. 6   Preference of ports

Cl. 7   *Expenditures of public money*

Cl. 8   Titles of nobility; presents from foreign State

§ 10

Cl. 1   *Powers denied States; treaties; money; ex post facto laws; obligation contracts*

Cl. 2   Imposts or duties

Cl. 3   Tonnage; State compacts; war

Art. II

§ 1

    Cl. 1   President; tenure

    Cl. 2   Presidential electors

    Cl. 3   Election of President and Vice President

    Cl. 4   Election day

    Cl. 5   Eligibility for office of President

    Cl. 6   Succession to office of President

    Cl. 7   Compensation of President

    Cl. 8   Oath of office

§ 2

    Cl. 1   *Commander in Chief; opinions of department heads; reprieves and pardons*

    Cl. 2   *Treaties; appointment of officers*

    Cl. 3   *Appointments during recess of Senate*

§ 3   Recommendations to Congress; convene and adjourn Congress; receive ambassadors; execute laws; and commission officers

§ 4   *Removal from office; impeachment; treason; bribery or other high crimes and misdemeanors*

Art. III

§ 1   Supreme Court and inferior courts; judges and compensation

§ 2

    Cl. 1   *Subjects of jurisdiction*

    Cl. 2   *Jurisdiction of Supreme Court*

    Cl. 3   *Trial by jury*

§ 3

    Cl. 1   Treason

    Cl. 2   Punishment of treason

Art. IV

§ 1   *Full faith and credit*

§ 2

    Cl. 1   *Privileges and immunities of citizens*

    Cl. 2   Delivery of fugitives

    Cl. 3   Runaway slaves

§ 3

    Cl. 1   Admission of new States

    Cl. 2   Territory or property of United States

§ 4   Form of State governments; protection

Art. V   Amendment of Constitution

Art. VI

§ 1

     Cl. 1   Prior debts valid under Constitution

     Cl. 2   *Supreme law; (Supremacy Clause)*

     Cl. 3   Oath of office

Art. VII *Ratification of Constitution*

AMENDMENTS

Amendment 1   *Religious and political freedom*

Amendment 2   *Right to bear arms*

Amendment 3   Quartering soldiers

Amendment 4   *Unreasonable searches and seizures*

Amendment 5   *Criminal actions; provisions concerning due process of law and just compensation clauses*

Amendment 6   *Rights of the accused*

Amendment 7   *Trial by jury in civil cases*

Amendment 8   Bail-punishment

Amendment 9   Rights retained by people

Amendment 10   *Powers reserved to the States or people*

Amendment 11   *Suits against States; restriction of judicial power*

Amendment 12   Election of President and Vice-President

Amendment 13   § 1   *Slavery prohibited*

                   § 2   Power to enforce amendment

Amendment 14   § 1   *Citizens of the United States*

                   § 2   Representatives; power to reduce apportionment

                   § 3   Disqualification to hold office

                   § 4   Public debt not to be questioned; debts of the Confederacy not to be paid

                   § 5   Power to enforce amendment

Amendment 15   § 1   *Right of citizens to vote; race or color not to disqualify*

                   § 2   Power to enforce amendment

Amendment 16   *Power to lay and collect taxes*

Amendment 17   Composition of the Senate

Amendment 18   § 1   National prohibition; intoxicating liquors

                   § 2   Concurrent power to enforce amendment

                   § 3   Time for adoption

Amendment 19   § 1   Woman suffrage; right to vote

                   § 2   Power to enforce amendment

Amendment 20   § 1   Executive and legislative departments; terms of elective officers

                   § 2   Annual meeting of Congress; date

                   § 3   Succession to office of President or Vice President

                   § 4   Death of President or Vice-President; selection of successor; choice of devolving on either house

                   § 5   Effective date of amendment

                   § 6   Time for ratification

Amendment 21   § 1   Repeal of Eighteenth Amendment

                   § 2   Intoxicating liquors; shipment into dry territory prohibited

                   § 3   Ratification; time limit

Amendment 22   § 1   Terms of office of the President
                § 2   Ratification

Amendment 23   § 1   Representatives in the electoral college to the District of Columbia
                § 2   Enforcement

Amendment 24   § 1   Qualification of electors
                § 2   Enforcement

Amendment 25   § 1   Succession to office of President
                § 2   Succession to office of Vice-President
                § 3   Declaration by President of inability to serve
                § 4   Declaration by others of President's inability to serve

Amendment 26   § 1   Eighteen year old voting rights
                § 2   Enforcement

Amendment 27   No law varying the compensation of Senators or Representatives shall take effect until an election of Representatives has intervened.

Exhibit 3: Agency and Partnership Table

(See p. 59)

Legend: GP = General Partnership; P = Partner; J&S = Joint and Several

AGENCY		
Creation	1) Oral or written agreement that Agent will act for Principal 2) Agent must act on behalf of Principal 3) Agent subject to control of Principal	
Sources of Authority	Actual or apparent authority	
Fiduciary Relationship	Duty of Loyalty	
Liability on Agent's Contract	Principal liable if Agent acts with authority. Agent liable if Principal undisclosed or unidentified.	
Liability for Agent's Torts	**Principal**	Vicarious Liability ("course and scope") Direct Liability—Principal failed to train/supervise; ratified contract
	Agent	Liable for own torts.

PARTNERSHIP ("P/S")			
	GP	**LP**	**LLP**
Filing Required	None	Statement of Qualification	Certificate of Ltd. P/S
Management Rights	Each P equal	Each P equal	Each Gen. P has equal right, Ltd. P has right to participate
Authority	Each P can bind P/S to extent of actual or apparent authority	Each P can bind P/S to extent of actual or apparent authority	Each P can bind P/S to extent of actual or apparent authority. Ltd. P can bind P/S but only so long as she has been authorized to do so.
Liability	J&S for P/S obligations	No J&S liability. Each P's capital contributions at risk.	Each Gen. P's capital contributions **and** personal assets at risk. Each Ltd. P's capital contributions at risk.
Distributions	Share equally	Share equally	Shared in relation to P's total contributions to P/S

Exhibit 4: MRPC Professional Responsibilities Rules Table

RULE	SUBJECT	DESCRIPTION
CLIENT-LAWYER RELATIONSHIP		
1.1	Competence	Must represent the client with the legal knowledge, skill, thoroughness and preparation reasonably necessary for the representation. Can gain competence through self-study or associating other counsel.
1.2	Scope of Representation	Must abide by client's decisions re: representation, can limit with informed consent. Exceptions are criminal or fraudulent conduct. Must write an engagement letter. Must follow client's objectives regarding means of achieving objectives. Client decides settlement or appeal; criminal decides pleas, demanding or waiving jury trial, and testifying at trial. Lawyer may withdraw pursuant to fundamental disagreement. Client controls objectives of representation; attorney controls means of achieving objectives.
1.3	Diligence	Must act with reasonable diligence and promptness in representing a client. Must show dedication and zeal and pursue to completion.
1.4	Communication	Must inform and consult with the client and promptly comply with requests to help the client make informed decisions. May delay if information would cause client to harm himself. Must inform client of settlement offers, orally is fine.
1.5	Fees	Must not make an arrangement for, charge, or collect an unreasonable fee or amount for expenses. Contingent fee arrangement must be in writing. No contingent fees for domestic or criminal cases. Can't advance more than litigation or court costs and may pay outright for indigent clients. May not split fees with other lawyers except: with lawyers in the same firm; former/retired lawyers per agreement; or with lawyers outside firm if fee is based on work performed. Client must consent in writing and the fee must be reasonable.
1.6	Confidentiality	Cannot reveal info relating to the representation without informed consent unless to prevent death or bodily harm. May reveal to the extent the lawyer reasonably believes necessary to follow a court order or other law. If harm has already been done, lawyer can't tell. He can only tell if harm will be caused in the future.

1.7	Conflict of Interest	Cannot represent a client if the representation involves a concurrent conflict of interest. Even if conflict exists, lawyer may represent both clients if he can reasonably represent them. No client will assert a claim against another client in the same case and each client gives written, informed consent. Conflicts between current clients asserting claims against each other are not assentable. When lawyer is forced to withdraw from multiple representations he must withdraw from all clients unless all consent to him representing only one. Can consent to conflict in writing unless adversaries in litigation.
1.8	Conflict of Interest – Specifics	Cannot enter into a business transaction with a client or knowingly acquire an interest adverse to a client. Lawyer may, however, use a lien to secure payment. Can't contract to limit malpractice liability unless client has independent counsel. Can't settle malpractice claim without advising client to obtain counsel. Lawyer shall not solicit any substantial gift from a client for himself or his relatives unless the receiver of the gift is related to the client. Lawyer can be the executor of client's estate with informed written consent of the client. Can't establish literary or media rights agreement before ceasing representation. No sexual relationships with clients unless the relationship pre-dated the attorney-client relationship.
1.9	Duties to Former Clients	Lawyer, or Lawyer's firm, is prevented from representing a client against a former client in the same or substantially related matter.
1.10	Imputation	If associated with a firm, must not knowingly represent a client, nor may any of the lawyers in the firm, unless Lawyer leaves the firm.
1.11	Special Conflicts – Government	Former government Lawyer is prohibited from participating in matters he was personally and substantially involved in while with the government without written informed consent.
1.12	Former Judge or Neutral Party	Can't represent any party regarding the matter of the ADR absent written informed consent from all. Can't negotiate for employment with another party, except a law clerk who notifies judge.
1.13	Organization as Client	If Lawyer knows of an employee acting or planning to act in a way that violates a legal duty that will cause injury, he must proceed as necessary in the best interest of the organization. However, Lawyer can't reveal the information if he is conducting an investigation. Must report to the highest authority, and if that is unproductive go outside the organization.

1.14	Client Diminished Capacity	Lawyer has a duty to maintain normal relationship, but if client faces danger, Lawyer must take reasonably necessary protective measures.
1.15	Safekeeping Property	If Lawyer receives a settlement fee and an amount is in dispute, the Lawyer can pay out the undisputed amount but must retain disputed amount in trust until resolved. Must keep client's money separate from his own in a trust account (IOLTA). If holding a large sum for a long period, must put in an interest bearing account and give interest to the client.
1.16	Declining or Terminating	Lawyer should write non-engagement letter to client they have chosen not to represent. *Must* return any unused portion of retainer or advance of fee. If relationship ends, lawyer is fired, lawyer withdraws (*must* or *may* return). *Must* if disability, illegality, or ethical violation. *May* if the client persists in crime/fraud, used lawyer's services to commit a past crime; the objective is repugnant, financial hardship for the Lawyer, or other good cause. Must protect client's interest, provide reasonable notice, and time to find a new lawyer. Must return unearned fees, paper, and property.
1.17	Sale of Law Practice	Can sell a law practice if seller ceases to practice law or an area of law in a reasonable geographic area, or if the entire practice is sold to lawyers or a law firm. Notice must be provided to clients and the client is deemed to have accepted if no response occurs within 90 days.
1.18	Duties to Prospective Clients	Lawyer must: protect confidential information; protect prospective client's property; and use reasonable care in giving advice.
COUNSELOR		
2.1	Advisor	Must use independent judgment, and give honest, candid advice.
2.3	Evaluation – Use by 3rd Parties	Can refer to matters outside the law. Can recommend professional help. Can evaluate matter for non-client if reasonably believes with written consent.
2.4	Lawyer as 3rd Party Neutral	Lawyer shall not have ex parte communication with judge regarding pending or impending matter except for scheduling or for settlement purposes, or if a judge approaches.
ADVOCATE		
3.1	Meritorious Claims/Contentions	Lawyer must reject case if legal position or defense is factually or legally frivolous. Not frivolous: • Good faith argument under existing law or for changing

		existing law • To make claim: before all facts can be substantiated, assert position before discovery, or a claim that the lawyer doesn't believe will win. Criminal defense Lawyer may require a prosecutor to prove every element of the charge. Prosecutor must have probable cause.
3.2	Expediting Litigation	Lawyer has a duty to make reasonable efforts to expedite litigation, consistent with the interest of the client. Lawyer may seek a postponement if not habitual. Delaying causes disrepute to judiciary.
3.3	Candor Toward Tribunal	Lawyer shall not present evidence he knows to be false. Must take corrective action. Can decline to offer testimony believed to be false except in a criminal trial. Lawyer shall cite legal authority adverse to the client if it is not cited by opposing counsel and is known to the Lawyer. No duty to prevent adverse facts. Limited witness preparation is permitted. If Lawyer knows client is going to lie, he must: dissuade, withdraw, and disclose. Lawyer is allowed to present truthful portion of testimony in narrative style in some cases, but doesn't elicit testimony. Shall not offer testimony known to be false and may refuse to offer evidence reasonably believed to be false.
3.4	Fairness to Opposition	Lawyer shall not falsify evidence, help a witness testify falsely, nor offer a witness an illegal inducement. May advise person not to voluntarily give info of client, relative, or employee if the Lawyer reasonably believes it is in the witness' best interest and witness will not be harmed by withholding. Shall not assert personal knowledge or opinions of fact. Can't conceal evidence or tell others not to testify.
3.5	Impartiality/Decorum of Tribunal	Lawyer shall not influence judge through illegal means, communicate ex parte with judge or juror during the proceeding unless permitted by law, and can't speak with juror after jury is discharged.
3.6	Trial Publicity	Lawyer can't make an extrajudicial statement if he reasonably knows it will be made public and will have a substantial likelihood of affecting the trial. Lawyer can make statements that are factual, pleas for help, warnings if there is no danger to the public, or identity or other information required to assist in apprehending the suspect. Must take reasonable care.
3.7	Lawyer as Witness	Lawyer can't act as an advocate at trial if Lawyer is likely to be a necessary witness unless: uncontested matter; cost of legal services; substantial hardship to client.

3.8	Prosecutor Responsibilities	Must take reasonable efforts to advise of right to counsel and refrain from prosecuting a charge that the prosecutor knows is not supported by probable cause. Higher standard than civil. Shall not subpoena a Lawyer to testify about a client unless the information is not privileged, is critical and there is no other alternative. No ex parte communications and is subject to all restrictions as other lawyers.
3.9	Advocate in Non-judicial Role	In front of a legislative body must disclose the appearance as in a representative capacity in conformance with MRPC.

TRANSACTIONS WITH OTHER THAN CLIENTS

4.1	Truthfulness to Others	Must be truthful in material statements of fact. Lawyer may use puffery in negotiations just not lying about material statements of fact. Must not fail to disclose a material fact to avoid crime or fraud.
4.2	Communication with Represented Party	Shall not communicate with a represented opposing client without consent or court authorization. However, represented parties can communicate with each other.
4.3	Unrepresented Person	Lawyer can't say he is disinterested. Lawyer must advise that he is not looking out for their interests. Can't give advice except to obtain counsel.
4.4	Respect for 3rd Party Rights	Lawyer should reject case if client's motive is harassment. Must be a substantial purpose other than to embarrass, delay, or burden. Must promptly notify sender upon receipt of inadvertent information.

LAW FIRMS AND ASSOCIATIONS

5.1	Partners, Managers, Supervisors	Must make sure other Lawyers follow the MRPC, remedy misconduct when discovered, manage non-lawyer behavior, and not ratify misconduct. Responsible for subordinates.
5.2	Subordinate Lawyer	Responsible for own conduct. May be exempt if misconduct based on a reasonable resolution of an arguable question of duty by a supervisory lawyer.
5.3	Non-Lawyer Assistants	Lawyer must manage non-lawyer behavior.
5.4	Professional Independence	Can share fees with non-lawyer relating to deceased partners or lawyer's practice (Profit sharing, salaries, fee award, placement fees for temp agency). No partnership with non-lawyer if law is practiced.

5.5	Unauthorized Practice	Lawyer can't practice outside a state where he is licensed, set up an office, state or imply he is licensed to practice outside the state in which he is licensed, or help a non-lawyer practice without a license.
5.6	Restrictions on Right to Practice	Can't make an agreement or settlement that limits the rights of an attorney to practice law except for a retirement agreement (It would limit a client's freedom to choose an attorney).
5.7	Law-Related Services	Provided by the Lawyer not distinct from provision of legal services. Must take reasonable measures to inform that the services are not legal services and the lawyer-client protection does not exist.
PUBLIC SERVICE		
6.1	Pro Bono Service	Should give 50 pro bono hours per year. (Note: there is no disciplinary action for failing to do so)
6.2	Accepting Appointments	Lawyer can only avoid court appointment for good cause, unreasonable financial burden, strong personal feelings, or impaired mental or physical condition.
6.3	Legal Services Organizations	Can serve as officer, but shall not participate in a decision of the LSO if it would be incompatible with obligations to regular client or would adversely affect LSO client.
6.4	Law Reform Activities	Can participate in law reform even if it harms client. If client benefitted, must disclose that fact, but not identify client.
6.5	Nonprofit Legal Services	Must obtain client's consent to limited scope of relationship and advise client to obtain further legal help if needed, if expected to proceed beyond the quick advice stage.
INFORMATION ABOUT LEGAL SERVICES		
7.1	Communications Re: Services	Lawyer can't make false or misleading statements or omit facts.
7.2	Advertising	Reciprocal referral agreement with another lawyer: not exclusive; client informed; not indefinite. Must include a lawyer's or firm's name and address. Must have consent to use client's name. Can't give anything of value for referral.
7.3	Solicitation of Clients	Can't make phone calls, in-person contact, or electronic contact to secure clients for pecuniary gain, except: lawyers, family, close friends, or prior clients. No contact if person has requested not to be contacted, or contact involves coercion, duress, or harassment. Written advertising must say "advertising material" on envelope. Electronic advertising material must contain "advertising material" on top and bottom.

7.4	Communication re: Practice	Can't say specialist if not certified by accredited or bar-approved organization. Must name the organization.
7.5	Firm Names/Letterheads	Can't use false or misleading name. Can use trade names if they don't suggest connection with charitable, public, or government organization. May use name in multiple States, but must state lawyer names and States admitted. If lawyer holds a public office, the firm may not use his name while he is not practicing law.
7.6	Political Contributions	Can't make a contribution for the purpose of obtaining an engagement or appointment.
MAINTAINING THE INTEGRITY OF THE PROFESSION		
8.1	Bar Admission/Discipline	Prohibits applicants from knowingly misstating an important fact. Requires correction of mistaken impressions.
8.2	Judicial/Legal Officials	Lawyer must not make reckless or false statement concerning qualifications or integrity of a judge, adjudicatory officer, public legal officer, or candidate for legal appointment or office.
1.3	Reporting Misconduct	Lawyer is required to report if he knows another lawyer or judge has knowingly violated the MRPC in a way that raises a substantial question of honesty, trustworthiness, or fitness as a lawyer.
8.4	Misconduct	Lawyer can't violate MRPC; commit a crime; engage in dishonesty, fraud, deceit, or misrepresentation; engage in conduct prejudicial to justice, state ability to influence officials; or assist a judge in doing so.
8.5	Disciplinary Authority Choice of Law	Lawyer may be disciplines by more than one jurisdiction for the same conduct, and is controlled by jurisdiction where the litigation is pending.
NOTE		
1	Lawyer Sanctions	Disbarment, suspension, reprimand, admonition
2	Attorney Speech	May be regulated if government has substantial interest, the restriction will advance that interest, and it is narrowly tailored.
JUDICIAL ETHICS (Model Code of Judicial Conduct)		
1.1		Shall comply with the law.
1.2		Shall act to promote public confidence in the independence, integrity, and impartiality of the judiciary and avoid the appearance of impropriety.
1.3		Must not abuse office to advance judge's own personal or economic interests. Can use letterhead for references if based on personal knowledge and not seen as pressuring.

2.1		Duties of judicial office shall take precedence over personal/extrajudicial activities.
2.2		Shall perform all duties fairly and impartially.
2.3		Shall avoid bias or prejudice and require lawyers in front of them to do the same.
2.4		Must not be swayed by public opinion or fear.
2.6		Shall allow litigants to be heard. May encourage settlement but not coerce it.
2.7		Must hear all matters assigned unless disqualified.
2.8		Shall require order and decorum in the courtroom and be patient and courteous
2.9		Must avoid ex parte communications and not independently investigate
2.10		Shall not make a public statement on pending cases.
2.11		Shall disqualify himself if impartiality questioned, 3rd degree relationships (great-grandparent, grandparent, parent, uncle, aunt, brother, sister, child, grandchild, great-grandchild, nephew, niece, cousin)
2.14		Must take action if he suspects impairment and make confidential referral to lawyer assistance program.
2.15		Must inform authorities if lawyer or judge violates rules.
3.1		No activities that interfere with judicial performance, frequently disqualify, undermine integrity or impartiality. Can't appear coercive or abuse court resources.
3.2		Shall not voluntarily appear at public hearings unless on matter re: acting pro se on personal matters, acting as fiduciary, or in the course of judicial activities.
3.3		Shall not testify as character witness unless subpoenaed.
3.4		Shall not accept appointment to government committee or commission that does not relate to the law.
3.6		Shall not be a member of discriminatory organization
3.7		Limitations on charitable or civic organizations. Okay: Law, legal, judiciary, non-profits (education, charities, fraternal groups)
3.8		Shall not accept appointment as fiduciary.
3.9		Shall not act as ADR neutral.
3.10		Shall not practice law.

3.11		May not serve as officer or employee of a business except family investments and family business if it doesn't jeopardize his position.
3.12		Reasonable compensation permitted unless it undermines independence.
3.13		Shall not accept gifts undermining judge's independence, integrity, or impartiality. Small things okay. Must report anything of value.
4.1		Shall not be connected with political campaigns or make false or misleading statements.
4.2		For elected judgeships, can establish campaign committee, make speeches, endorse, and make contributions.
4.3		For appointed judges, can communicate with appointing body and seek endorsements other than from partisan political organizations.
4.5		Must resign from bench if becoming candidate for elected office.

Glossary

ABA	American Bar Association
Accord and Satisfaction	A later agreement changing the terms of the original agreement, to which both parties agree.
Actus Reus	A guilty act; a physical act or an unlawful omission.
Ad Valorem	According to its value; generally used for real property.
Ademption	The remedy for when a specific devise no longer exists.
Ameliorative	In terms of property waste, ameliorative "adds" value.
Arguendo	In arguing.
Ascertainable	In terms of beneficiaries, those that are identifiable.
Asportation	Moving of personal property, even an inch
Barbri	A Dallas-based corporation that produces education materials.
BARRK	General Intent crimes: burglary, arson, rape, robbery, and kidnapping.
Beneficiaries	Recipients of the res of a trust.
Bequeath	A gift of personal property, left by the deceased.
BFP	Bona fide purchaser, sometimes BFPV (…for value).
BITC	In family law, the best interests of the child.
Bona Fide	True, honest, or genuine; acted based on good faith.
Bridge-the-gap	Alimony that eases the transition between married and single life, generally not exceeding two years.
Capacity	A person's ability to enter into a contract, go to trial, commit a crime, etc.
Caveat emptor	Buyer beware.
Certiorari	Review, generally by the Supreme Court.
Charitable trust	A trust for charitable purpose that benefits the public. It does not require ascertainable beneficiaries.
Chattel	Personal property.
CRAMM BAR SLAB	Specific Intent Crimes: conspiracy, rape, assault, murder, manslaughter, burglary, arson, robbery, solicitation, larceny, attempt, and battery.
Cunningham Test	A capacity test regarding a testator understanding the nature of his disposition and the extent of his property.

Cy pres	A doctrine that allows the court to allocate trust funds for purposes not expressed in the trust in an attempt to carry out the settlor's intent.
De facto	As a matter of fact.
De minimis	Insignificant or minimal importance.
De novo	New, fresh look.
Devise	A gift in real property, left by the deceased.
Devisee	Person receiving a gift of real property.
Dicta	(plural) Said in passing; opinions or comments. (*singular* form is "dictum")
DPC	Due Process Clause
Duces Tecum	Subpoena; or request for production meaning, "bring it with you."
Durational	Alimony for a specific period of time, generally not exceeding the length of the marriage.
Durham Test	When a defendant proves that his crime was a product of his mental illness.
En banc	A panel of judges
Enjoin	To have stopped; obtain an injunction.
Enumerated	Written and numbered.
EPC	Equal Protection Clause
Equitable distribution	Method of distributing marital property.
Estoppel	To have stopped.
Ex parte	A proceeding taken for the benefit of one party.
Ex post facto	After the fact; a retroactive law that affects a prior case.
Exigent	Emergency and extenuating (circumstances).
Express	Written
Forum	Generally, the appropriate court.
Forum non conveniens	Doctrine allowing the transfer of cases to a court that would be more convenient based on the location of the witnesses, evidence, accident, etc.
FRCP	Federal Rules of Civil Procedure
Guardian ad litem	Person appointed by the court to protect the interests of someone else, generally a child or elderly person.

Habeas Corpus	"You have the body"; Generally pertains to a writ of habeas corpus demanding that a detained person be brought before the court.
Hearsay	Generally, anything said outside of court.
IICDUM	Contract defenses: impracticability, impracticability, capacity, duress, unconscionability, and mistake.
IIED	Intentional infliction of emotional distress.
Implied	Not written but understood based on intent or common course of dealings.
In camera	In private or in chambers to protect privacy or confidentiality.
In personam	Against the person; court's jurisdiction over the person.
In re	In relation to or in the matter of.
In rem	An action taken directly against property.
Insane Delusions Test	A test to determine lack of capacity in a testator. Insane delusions must materially affect the disposition of the will.
Inter alia	"Among other things"
Inter vivos	Made between the living.
Irresistible Impulse Test	An insanity test that states that the defendant was unable to control his actions or conform to the law.
Issuance	When a corporation sells its own shares.
JMOL	Judgment as a Matter of Law
JNOV	Judgment Non Obstante Veredicto (or "Judgment notwithstanding the verdict")
Laches	An affirmative defense meaning "slept on your rights".
LLC	Limited Liability Corporation
LLLP	Limited Liability Limited Partnership
LLP	Limited Liability Partnership
LP	Limited Partnership
LSIB	*Law School "In-Brief"*, the "mother text" to this book, which examines Federal law for the various subjects.
Mandamus	"We command"
MBE	Multistate Bar Examination
M'Naghten Test	A disease of the mind that caused a defect of reason, such that the defendant lacked the ability to know the wrongfulness of his act or to understand his actions.

Mens Rea	A guilty mind or criminal intent.
Miranda Warnings	Notice that: a person has the right to remain silent; anything they say can and will be used against them in a court of law; they have a right to counsel; and if they can't afford counsel, counsel will be provided for them. To read these warning to a suspect means they have been "Mirandized."
MOIPKKIA	(Character Evidence) Motive; Opportunity; Intent; Preparation; Plan; Knowledge; Identity; and Absence of mistake.
MOL	Memorandum of Law
Moot	Generally, when a cause of action for which a lawsuit was filed no longer exists, or has been remedied.
MPC	Model Penal Code insanity test stating that the defendant lacked substantial capacity to appreciate the criminality of his act or to conform his conduct to the law.
MPRE	Multistate Professional Responsibilities Exam
MPT	Multistate Performance Test
MRPC	Model Rules of Professional Conduct
MSJ	Motion for Summary Judgment
MTD	Motion to Dismiss
MY LEGS	Required by the Statute of Frauds: Marriage; agreement longer than one Year; agreement for Land, Executory agreement; Goods over $500; and Suretyship agreements.
NCBE	National Conference of Bar Examiners
NIED	Negligent Infliction of Emotional Distress
NMR	Non-Monetary Remedies.
NOV	Non Obstante Veredicto, notwithstanding the verdict.
Novation	A new agreement
Outstanding shares	Issued shares that have not been reacquired by a corporation.
Par value	Minimum issuance price, not the fair market value.
Parol	(Evidence) Extrinsic, written, or oral.
Partnership	An association of two or more persons carrying on as co-owners of a business for profit.
Past recollection recorded	A writing that is substituted for memory.
Pendente Lite	Alimony during litigation.

Per autre vie	For or during another person's life. In terms of property, an estate that terminates on the death of someone other than the grantee.
Per capita	"By the head." Beneficiaries take equally.
Per curiam	Decision made by the court with no stated author.
Per se	Inherently, or in itself.
Per stirpes	By representation. (Wills) Where heirs divide property among themselves versus where they take under the will.
Permanent	Alimony that is determined according to the length of the marriage.
Precedent	A binding decision previously made by a court.
Present recollection revived	(Evidence) Where a witness relates a present recollection.
Prima facie	On its face. Evidence is sufficient to establish a case on its face.
Private Trust	A trust with ascertainable beneficiaries, not for public benefit.
Probate	Property left by a decedent that passes by will or intestacy.
Process	Generally, service of process is a copy of complaint and summons.
Promissory Estoppel	Contracts remedy. Occurs when a promise is made by one party to another who relies on the promise to his detriment, and the person making the promise expected the reliance. Injustice can be avoided only by enforcing the promise.
Prudent Trustee Rule	(Trusts) A trustee should: abide by the statute; take into account probable income; and protect the principal of the trust. Trustee should diversify in investing trust funds and not engage in self-dealing. (see "Trustee).
Punitive	Damages meant to punish, not compensate.
Quantum Meruit	"As much as he deserves." (Contracts) Recovery based on unjust enrichment. Generally, the reasonable value of services or materials furnished under a contract.
Quasi	Means "almost like".
RAP	Rule against perpetuities.
Recorded Recollection	Where a witness is unable to remember and her own writing may be admitted in place of her testimony.
Rehabilitative	Alimony for one spouse who sacrificed his/her career for the spouse's career. The goal is to enable him/her to enhance skills to reenter the job market. Generally, not for more than three years.

Remand	Generally, where a higher court sends a case back to a lower court to reevaluate the case with specific directions.
Res ipsa loquitur	"Speaks for itself." Generally extends a rebuttable presumption of negligence for certain actions.
Res judicata	A decision that has already been made. Generally when a court has rendered a final judgment on the merits, it prevents the parties of the case from revisiting the issues.
Respondeat Superior	Literally means "Let the master reply." In torts, it is where an employer is liable for the actions of his employee.
Reverse	When a court overturns a decision of a lower court.
Revocation	When a party to a contract revokes an offer prior to it being accepted.
Ripe	When a law is in question, but no harm has yet been done. Effectively, no case or controversy exists to be heard.
RPP	Reasonably prudent person
SBI	Serious bodily injury
SCOTUS	Supreme Court of the United States
Service	The act of serving a complaint and summons according to statutory guidelines.
Settlor	A person who establishes a trust.
SMJ	Subject matter jurisdiction
SOF	Statute of Frauds
Stare decisis	"To stand by that which has been decided."
Sua sponte	"Of its own will." Where a court decides something in its own discretion.
TBE	Tenancy-by-the-entirety.
Testator	A person who creates a will.
Trust	Legal title to property held by one party for the benefit of another. Trustees have legal title, beneficiaries have equitable title.
Trustee	A person appointed as responsible for administering a trust. (*see* "Prudent Trustee Rule")
UBE	Uniform Bar Examination
UCC	Uniform Commercial Code

Undue Influence	A concept relating to capacity in wills to determine if a person was under undue influence when he created the will. Courts looks for: a confidential relationship; caretaking; a close relationship; signs of transportation or medical care provided; joint accounts; physical or mental weakness; advanced age; and power of attorney.
Unenumerated	Unwritten, implied. In terms of Constitutional Law, this refers to rights that are not expressly written in the Constitution; e.g. marriage, abortion, etc.
UPC	Uniform Probate Code
UTC	Uniform Trust Code
Vacate	Generally when a higher court erases a lower court's decision so that it will not be relied on as precedent.
Vacatur	The doctrine of vacating a case.
Venue	The proper location of the forum.
Vicarious liability	A doctrine where the employer or an agent becomes liable for the act of his employees or those acting under the agent's authority.
Voir dire	The process of selecting jurors, generally to eliminate bias or prejudice
Watered stock	Stock that is purchased for less than par value.
Writ	A petition. Generally used in reference to: writ of certiorari; writ of habeas corpus; or writ of mandamus.

About the Authors

Glenn has a combined 45 years of experience in the military, intelligence and private sector arenas and has held positions of increasing responsibility to include the position of CEO. Please feel free to view his LinkedIn Profile for more details. Email him at inbriefseries@gmail.com.

Jackson graduated from the Virginia Military Institute and worked as a law enforcement officer in his native Maryland. This is his first contribution to the "In-Brief"® series.

Both authors hold Juris Doctor degrees from the Florida Coastal School of Law.

Made in the USA
Columbia, SC
20 January 2022